ABRAHAM LINCOLN'S SPEECHES.

COMPILED BY

L. E. CHITTENDEN,

Ex-Register of the Treasury,

AUTHOR OF "PRESIDENT LINCOLN," "PERSONAL
REMINISCENCES," ETC.

NEW YORK
B. W. DODGE & COMPANY
PUBLISHERS

CONTENTS.

INTRODUCTION.

THE memory of ABRAHAM LINCOLN grows dearer to his countrymen with lapse of time. The more thorough study of his writings, and a higher appreciation of his public services, may involve a revision of some opinions founded upon imperfect or unreliable evidence, but they will lead no one to admire or love him less. It seems to be the desire of true Americans to know him just as he was.

No more valuable contribution to an accurate knowledge of Abraham Lincoln could be made, than a proper selection from his speeches and writings, in a single volume of convenient, readable form; and no book of that kind could be more difficult to make. His collected works, including his speeches in Congress, his political debates, and his official papers, would fill several large volumes. Upon what principle or by what rule shall they be compressed into a duodecimo of three or four hundred pages, which will hold the interest of the reader, and enable him to form an accurate estimate of their great author and the true lessons of his life and pen?

The compilation which I have made will be better understood by a statement of some of the facts of his early life. I shall give these facts as I understand them, without citing authorities. Doubtless there are those who will controvert them, with whom I shall here have no dispute. As I give them, they are consistent with his character, and the evidence is open to those who wish to examine it further.

Abraham Lincoln, born in Kentucky, was descended from a New England ancestry, from which he inherited an intense love of liberty, thoroughness of character, and perfect integrity. As often happens, these qualities did not appear in his father, who was poor, improvident, and ignorant. His mother was an energetic Christian woman of much refinement, whose devotion to her domestic and maternal duties soon wore out her frail body, but imprinted her image indelibly upon the heart of her son. Many times he said that all he was, he owed to her. Then it may be assumed that to her he owed his rugged honesty, which became a part of his name, and that thoroughness which led him to commit much of the Bible to memory, and which lay at the foundation of his success. He did with his might whatever his hand found to do. Born to poverty, without paternal direction, he turned from one avocation to another, until he became a lawyer, entered public life, and was elected to Congress. From 1848, when he declined a re-election to Congress, to June, 1858, he scarcely challenged public notice. He made a speech at Peoria in 1854, and a few addresses in the Fremont campaign, but during those ten years he was not in public life, nor a candidate for office.

The period of his apparent inaction was that of the metamorphosis of slavery. It comprised the repeal of the Missouri Compromise, the Dred Scott decision, and the warfare in Kansas and Nebraska. What he was doing all this time is evident from his subsequent life.

From that source we learn that he must have been diligently engaged in the study of the history of American slavery. He saw in it the great question of the time, upon which depended the perpetuity of the Union. Slavery had previously been patient under restriction, — it had consented to the several compromises. Now it had suddenly become aggressive, and not only demanded the repeal of those compromises, but the affirmation of its right to enter any Territory of the United States. In defiance of their constitutions, it even threatened to claim recognition in the States which were supposed to have been appropriated in perpetuity to freedom.

Mr. Lincoln began his study of slavery with the adoption of the Federal Constitution, the commencement of its legislative history. The thoroughness of his investigations may be seen in his Cooper Institute speech in New York (February, 1860), wherein he traced the opinions of a majority of the members of the first Constitutional Convention on the subject of slavery. Step by step he followed that history, — there was no public man whose votes or speeches escaped his search. Finally he reached the conclusion which made him the President of the United States, the destroyer of the institution, and the emancipator of a race.

That conclusion was, that the free and the slave States had lived harmoniously together for eighty years, *because* the framers of the Constitution, the statesmen who succeeded them, and the public mind during all that time had rested in the belief that slavery was in the course of ultimate extinction, and would finally come to a peaceful end. Therefore they had consented to the abolition of the African slave-trade and other restrictions without objection.

But a great change had taken place. The advocates of slavery in the South, and their allies in the North, now claimed that slavery should be fostered and made a permanent institution ; that property in slaves, like any other property, was entitled to be taken into any Territory of the United States, and to be protected there ; that the Missouri Compromise must be repealed, and all other restrictions removed. These claims involved the further claim that slave property should be protected, and consequently that slavery should be lawful in all the free States of the Union.

Mr. Lincoln knew that the free States would never consent to these changes. The differences between them and the teachers of the new school were radical. The free States held that the clause in the Declaration of Independence that all men were created equal, included the negro, and that to enslave him was to commit a moral and political wrong. The South held that slavery was morally and politically right. The surrender of its opinions was prohibited by the conscience of the North ; the South would not give up its claim. The two could not live

together. The country must become all slave
or all free, or the free and the slave States must
separate.

All this was as clear as the sunlight to the eye
of Abraham Lincoln when, on the 16th of June,
1858, in the convention which nominated him to
the Senate of the United States, he discoursed
from the text, " If a house be divided against
itself, that house cannot stand," and declared his
belief that this government could not permanently
endure half slave and half free. It was useless
for his friends to remonstrate ; to assure him
that he would be charged with fomenting a sectional war ; to entreat him to modify or to withdraw that statement. He simply could not. It
was the truth, plain and unclouded ; he might,
with his party, fall and perish, but he could not
be disloyal to the truth.

From this time to his nomination for the Presidency — covering a very important period of his
life, comprising the debate with Judge Douglas
and many of his most powerful speeches — almost all his public utterances, varied, logical, and
powerful as they are, cluster about and illustrate
the foregoing text and its associations. It may
seem to some unnecessary to multiply extracts
from them. Slavery is dead. It will no more

disturb our peace. It has none but an historical interest for the present generation. Why, then, repeat arguments which have spent their force, and demonstrations which have accomplished their purpose?

There are still some survivors of the past who, with the writer, remember what an inspiration to patriotism these arguments were when slavery was making ready to raise its hand against the ark of our covenant. They relate to one of the eras in the history of our Republic. They cannot be too well known to the present generation or its posterity. It is better to incur some charge of repetition than to lose the memory of their eloquence and power.

The opinion has prevailed that the youth of Abraham Lincoln gave small promise of his future eminence, — that his intellectual powers were slow in reaching their maturity. Such an opinion needs revision. His address to the people of Sangamon County, at the age of twenty-three, and that before the Lyceum at Springfield three years later, give as full promise as could be expected at that age, of the speech at Gettysburg and the two inaugural addresses.

I shall not attempt any criticism of the power or excellence of the following extracts, nor any defence of their selection. They have been made after a thorough study of Mr. Lincoln's intellectual life, from its commencement to its close. If it shall occur to any that omissions have been made, — as, for example, in the great debate with Senator Douglas, — it should be remembered that this book is not a history. It is a collection intended to comprise the best expressions of a great patriot, perhaps the greatest patriot-statesman who has honoured our Republic since its birth. If by its publication I shall succeed in making him better known to the Republic he did so much to preserve, and to the people in whose service his life was sacrificed, I shall feel that I have been adequately rewarded.

ABRAHAM LINCOLN.

ADDRESS TO THE PEOPLE OF SANGAMON COUNTY.[1]

NEW SALEM, *March* 9, 1832.

TO THE PEOPLE OF SANGAMON COUNTY:

FELLOW-CITIZENS, — Having become a candidate for the honourable office of one of your Representatives in the next General Assembly of this State, in accordance with an established custom and the principles of true republicanism, it becomes my duty to make known to you, the people whom I propose to represent, my sentiments with regard to local affairs.

---

[1] Interest is attached to this Address from the fact that it is the earliest-known product of Mr. Lincoln's pen. It was issued when, at the age of twenty-three, he was first a candidate for the office of Representative to the Legislature of Illinois. It is therefore given without abbreviation. Mr. Lincoln was defeated. He was running on the opposition ticket to General Jackson, the popular Presidential candidate in Illinois.

Time and experience have verified to a demonstration the public utility of internal improvements. That the poorest and most thinly populated countries would be greatly benefited by the opening of good roads and in the clearing of navigable streams within their limits, is what no person will deny. Yet it is folly to undertake works of this or any other kind, without first knowing that we are able to finish them, — as half-finished work generally proves to be labour lost.

There cannot justly be any objection to having railroads and canals, any more than to other good things, provided they cost nothing. The only objection is to paying for them ; and the objection arises from the want of ability to pay.

With respect to the County of Sangamon, some more easy means of communication than it now possesses, for the purpose of facilitating the task of exporting the surplus products of its fertile soil, and importing necessary articles from abroad, are indispensably necessary. A meeting has been held of the citizens of Jacksonville and the adjacent country for the purpose of deliberating and inquiring into the expediency of constructing a railroad from some eligible point on the Illinois River through the town of Jacksonville, in Morgan County, to the town of Springfield, in Sangamon County. This is, indeed, a very desirable object. No other improvement that reason will justify us in hoping for can equal in utility the railroad. It is a never-failing source of communication between places of business remotely situated from each other. Upon the railroad the regular progress of commercial intercourse is not interrupted by either high or low water, or freezing weather, which are the principal difficulties that render our future hopes of water communication precarious and uncertain.

Yet, however desirable an object the construction of a railroad through our country may be; however high our imaginations may be heated at thoughts of it; there is always a heart-appalling shock accompanying the account of its cost which forces us to shrink from our pleasing anticipations. The probable cost of this contemplated railroad is estimated at $290,000; the bare statement of which, in my opinion, is sufficient to justify the belief that the improvement of the Sangamon River is an object much better suited to our infant resources.

Respecting this view, I think I may say, without the fear of being contradicted, that its navigation may be rendered completely practicable as high as the mouth of the South Fork, or probably higher, to vessels of from twenty-five to thirty tons' burden, for at least one half of all common years, and to vessels of much greater burden a part of the time. From my peculiar circumstances, it is probable that for the last twelve months I have given as particular attention to the stage of the water in this river as any other person in the country. In the month of March, 1831, in company with others, I commenced the building of a flat-boat on the Sangamon, and finished and took her out in the course of the spring. Since that time I have been concerned in the mill at New Salem. These circumstances are sufficient evidence that I have not been very inattentive to the stages of the water. The time at which we crossed the mill-dam being in the last days of April, the water was lower than it had been since the breaking of winter in February, or than it was for several weeks after. The principal difficulties we encountered in descending the river were from the drifted timber, which obstructions all know are not difficult to be removed. Knowing almost precisely the height of water at that time, I believe I am safe in saying that it has as often been higher as lower since.

From this view of the subject, it appears that my calculations with regard to the navigation of the Sangamon cannot but be founded in reason; but whatever may be its natural advantages, certain it is that it never can be practically useful to any great extent without being greatly improved by art. The drifted timber, as I have before mentioned, is the most formidable barrier to this object. Of all parts of the river, none will require so much labour in proportion to make it navigable as the last thirty or thirty-five miles; and going with the meanderings of the channel, when we are this distance above its mouth, we are only between twelve and eighteen miles above Beardstown, in something near a straight direction, and this route is upon such low ground as to retain water in many places during the season, and in all parts such as to draw two-thirds or three-fourths of the river-water at all high stages.

This route is on prairie-land the whole distance, so that it appears to me, by removing the turf a sufficient width and damming up the old channel, the whole river in a short time would wash its way through, thereby curtailing the distance and increasing the velocity of the current very considerably, while there would be no timber on the banks to obstruct its navigation in future; and, being nearly straight, the timber which might float in at the head would be apt to go clear through. There are also many places above this where the river, in its zigzag course, forms such complete peninsulas as to be easier to cut at the necks than to remove the obstructions from the bends, which, if done, would also lessen the distance.

What the cost of this work would be I am unable to say. It is probable, however, that it would not be greater than is common to streams of the same length. Finally, I believe the improvement of the Sangamon River to be vastly important and highly desirable to the people of the county, and, if elected, any measure in the Legislature having this for its object which may appear judicious, will meet my approbation and shall receive my support.

It appears that the practice of drawing [qu. loaning?] money at exorbitant rates of interest has already been opened as a field for discussion, so I suppose I may enter upon it without claiming the honour, or risking the danger, which may await its first explorer. It seems as though we were never to have an end to this baneful and corroding system, acting almost as prejudicially to the general interests of the community as a direct tax of several thousand dollars annually laid on each county for the benefit of a few individuals only, unless there be a law made fixing the limits of usury. A law for this purpose, I am of opinion, may be made without materially injuring any class of people. In cases of extreme necessity there could always be means found to cheat the law, while in all other cases it would have its intended effect. I would favour the passage of a law on this subject which might not be very easily evaded. Let it be such that the labour and difficulty of evading it could only be justified in cases of greatest necessity.

Upon the subject of education, not presuming to dictate any plan or system respecting it, I can only say that I view it as the most important subject which we, as a people, can be engaged in. That every man may receive at least a moderate education, and thereby be enabled to read the histories of his own and other countries, by which he may duly appreciate the value of our free institutions, appears to be an object of vital importance, even on this account alone, to say nothing of the advantages and satisfaction to be derived from all being able to read the Scriptures and other works, both of a religious and moral nature, for themselves.

For my part, I desire to see the time when education — and by its means morality, sobriety, enterprise, and industry — shall become much more general than at present; and should be gratified to have it in my power to contribute something to the advancement of any measure which might have a tendency to accelerate that happy period.

With regard to existing laws, some alterations are thought to be necessary. Many respectable men have suggested that our estray laws — the law respecting the issuing of executions, the road law, and some others — are deficient in their present form, and require alterations. But considering the great probability that the framers of those laws were wiser than myself, I should prefer not meddling with them, unless they were first attacked by others, in which case I should feel it both a privilege and a duty to take that stand which, in my view, might tend to the advancement of justice.

But, fellow-citizens, I shall conclude. Considering the great degree of modesty which should always attend youth, it is probable I have already been more presuming than becomes me. However, upon the subjects of which I have treated, I have spoken as I have thought. I may be wrong in regard to any or all of them; but, holding it a sound maxim that it is better only to be sometimes right than at all times wrong, so soon as I discover my opinions to be erroneous I shall be ready to renounce them.

Every man is said to have his peculiar ambition. Whether it be true or not, I can say, for one, that I have no other so great as that of being truly esteemed of my fellow-men by rendering myself worthy of their esteem. How far I shall succeed in gratifying this ambition is yet to be developed. I am young and unknown to many of you; I was born and have ever remained in the most humble walks of life. I have no wealthy or popular relations or friends to recommend me. My case is thrown exclusively upon the independent voters of the county, and if elected, they will have conferred a favour upon me for which I shall be unremitting in my labours to compensate. But if the good people in their wisdom shall see fit to keep me in the background, I have been too familiar with disappointments to be very much chagrined.

Your friend and fellow-citizen,

A. LINCOLN.

2

FROM HIS ADDRESS BEFORE THE YOUNG MEN'S
LYCEUM OF SPRINGFIELD, ILLINOIS, ON THE PER-
PETUATION OF OUR POLITICAL INSTITUTIONS.[1]

January, 1837.

" . . . In the great journal of things happen-
ing under the sun, we, the American people, find
our account running under the date of the nine-
teenth century of the Christian era. We find
ourselves in the peaceful possession of the fairest
portion of the earth, as regards extent of territory, fertility of soil, and salubrity of climate.
We find ourselves under the government of a
system of political institutions conducing more
essentially to the ends of civil and religious liberty, than any of which the history of former
times tells us. We, when remounting the stage
of existence, found ourselves the legal inheritors
of these fundamental blessings. We toiled not
in the acquirement or the establishment of them;
they are a legacy bequeathed to us by a once
hardy, brave, and patriotic, but now lamented
and departed race of ancestors.

"Theirs was the task (and nobly they performed
it) to possess themselves, and through themselves

---

[1] Published in the Springfield " Weekly Journal." See
Arnold's " Life of Lincoln," p. 61.

us, of this goodly land, and to rear upon its hills and valleys a political edifice of liberty and equal rights; 't is ours only to transmit these, — the former unprofaned by the foot of the invader; the latter undecayed by lapse of time. This, our duty to ourselves and to our posterity, and love for our species in general, imperatively require us to perform.

"How, then, shall we perform it? At what point shall we expect the approach of danger? By what means shall we fortify against it? Shall we expect some transatlantic military giant to step across the ocean and crush us at a blow? Never. All the armies of Europe, Asia, and Africa combined, with all the treasure of the earth (our own excepted) in their military chest, with a Bonaparte for a commander, could not, by force, take a drink from the Ohio, or make a track on the Blue Ridge, in a trial of a thousand years.

"At what point, then, is the approach of danger to be expected? I answer, if it ever reaches us, it must spring up among us. It cannot come from abroad. If destruction be our lot, we must ourselves be its author and finisher. As a nation of freemen, we must live through all time, or die by suicide.

" . . . There is even now something of ill

omen among us. I mean the increasing disregard for law which pervades the country; the growing disposition to substitute wild and furious passions in lieu of the sober judgment of courts; and the worse than savage mobs for the executive ministers of justice. This disposition is awfully fearful in any community; and that it now exists in ours, though grating to our feelings to admit, it would be a violation of truth and an insult to our intelligence to deny.

.   .   .   .

"I know the American people are *much* attached to their government. I know they would suffer *much* for its sake. I know they would endure evils long and patiently before they would ever think of exchanging it for another. Yet, notwithstanding all this, if the laws be continually despised and disregarded, if their rights to be secure in their persons and property are held by no better tenure than the caprice of a mob, the alienation of their affection for the government is the natural consequence, and to that sooner or later it must come.

"Here, then, is one point at which danger may be expected. The question recurs, how shall we fortify against it? The answer is simple. Let every American, every lover of liberty, every

well-wisher to his posterity, swear by the blood of
the Revolution never to violate in the least particular the laws of the country, and never to tolerate
their violation by others. As the patriots of seventy-six did to the support of the Declaration of
Independence, so to the support of the Constitution and the Laws let every American pledge
his life, his property, and his sacred honour;
let every man remember that to violate the law
is to trample on the blood of his father, and to
tear the charter of his own and his children's
liberty. Let reverence for the laws be breathed
by every American mother to the lisping babe
that prattles on her lap. Let it be taught in
schools, in seminaries, and in colleges. Let it
be written in primers, spelling-books, and in
almanacs. Let it be preached from the pulpit,
proclaimed in legislative halls, and enforced in
courts of justice. And, in short, let it become
the political religion of the nation.

. . . .

"Many great and good men, sufficiently qualified for any task they should undertake, may ever
be found, whose ambition would aspire to nothing
beyond a seat in Congress, a gubernatorial or a
presidential chair. But such belong not to the

family of the lion or the brood of the eagle. What? Think you these places would satisfy an Alexander, a Cæsar, or a Napoleon? Never! Towering genius disdains a beaten path. It seeks regions hitherto unexplored. It sees no distinction in adding story to story upon the monuments of fame erected to the memory of others. It denies that it is glory enough to serve under any chief. It scorns to tread in the footsteps of any predecessor, however illustrious. It thirsts and burns for distinction; and, if possible, it will have it, whether at the expense of emancipating slaves, or enslaving free men. Is it unreasonable, then, to expect that some men, possessed of the loftiest genius, coupled with ambition sufficient to push it to its utmost stretch, will at some time spring up among us? And when such a one does, it will require the people to be united with each other, attached to the government and laws, and generally intelligent, to successfully frustrate his design.

" Distinction will be his paramount object, and although he would as willingly, perhaps more so, acquire it by doing good as harm, yet that opportunity being passed, and nothing left to be done in the way of building up, he would sit down boldly to the task of pulling down. Here, then, is a probable case, highly dangerous, and such a one as could not well have existed heretofore.

. . . .

"All honour to our Revolutionary ancestors, to whom we are indebted for these institutions. They will not be forgotten. In history we hope they will be read of, and recounted, so long as the Bible shall be read. But even granting that they will, their influence cannot be what it heretofore has been. Even then, they cannot be so universally known, nor so vividly felt, as they were by the generation just gone to rest. At the close of that struggle, nearly every adult male had been a participator in some of its scenes. The consequence was, that of those scenes, in the form of a husband, a father, a son, or a brother, a living history was to be found in every family, — a history bearing the indubitable testimonies to its own authenticity in the limbs mangled, in the scars of wounds received in the midst of the very scenes related; a history, too, that could be read and understood alike by all, the wise and the ignorant, the learned and the unlearned. But those histories are gone. They can be read no more for ever. They were a fortress of strength; but what the invading foemen could never do, the silent artillery of time has done, —

the levelling of its walls. They are gone. They were a forest of giant oaks; but the resistless hurricane has swept over them, and left only here and there a lonely trunk, despoiled of its verdure, shorn of its foliage, unshading and unshaded, to murmur in a few more gentle breezes, and to combat with its mutilated limbs a few more ruder storms, and then to sink and be no more. "

. . . .

MR. LINCOLN'S EARLIEST ANNOUNCEMENT OF HIS POLITICAL OPINIONS.

June, 1836, and *March,* 1837.

IN his letter published in the Sangamon " Journal," in June, 1836, he said : " I go for all sharing the privileges of the government who assist in bearing its burdens : consequently I go for admitting all whites to the right of suffrage who pay taxes or bear arms [by no means excluding females.] "

From his Protest in the Journal of the Legislature of Illinois, signed by Mr. Lincoln
and Dan Stone.

March, 1837.

"The undersigned believe that the institution
of slavery is founded on both injustice and bad
policy, but that the promulgation of abolition
doctrine tends rather to increase than to abate
its evils.

"They believe that the Congress of the United
States has no power under the Constitution to
interfere with the institution of slavery in the
different States.

"They believe that the Congress of the United
States has the power, under the Constitution, to
abolish slavery in the District of Columbia, but
that that power ought not to be exercised unless
at the request of the people of said district."

EXTRACTS FROM A POLITICAL DEBATE BETWEEN MR. LINCOLN, E. D. BAKER, AND OTHERS, AGAINST STEPHEN A. DOUGLAS, JOSIAH LAMBORN, AND OTHERS, HELD IN THE SECOND PRESBYTERIAN CHURCH IN SPRINGFIELD, ILLINOIS.

December, 1839.

IN concluding his speech, Mr. Lincoln said: "Mr. Lamborn insists that the difference between the Van Buren party and the Whigs is, that although the former sometimes err in practice, they are always correct in principle, whereas the latter are wrong in principle; and the better to impress this proposition, he uses a figurative expression in these words: 'The Democrats are vulnerable in the heel, but they are sound in the heart and in the head.' The first branch of the figure — that is, that the Democrats are vulnerable in the heel — I admit is not merely figuratively but literally true. Who that looks but for a moment at their Swartwouts, their Prices, their Harringtons, and their hundreds of others, scampering away with the public money to Texas, to Europe, and to every spot of the earth where a villain may hope to find refuge from justice, can at all doubt that they are most distressingly

affected in their heels with a species of running
fever? It seems that this malady of their heels
operates on the sound-headed and honest-hearted
creatures very much like the cork leg in the song
did on its owner, which, when he had once got
started on it, the more he tried to stop it, the
more it would run away. At the hazard of wear-
ing this point threadbare, I will relate an anec-
dote which seems to be too strikingly in point to
be omitted. A witty Irish soldier who was always
boasting of his bravery when no danger was near,
but who invariably retreated without orders at the
first charge of the engagement, being asked by
his captain why he did so, replied, ' Captain, I
have as brave a heart as Julius Cæsar ever had ;
but somehow or other, whenever danger approaches, my cowardly legs will run away with
it.' So it is with Mr. Lamborn's party. They
take the public money into their hands for the
most laudable purpose that wise heads and honest
hearts can dictate, but before they can possibly
get it out again, their rascally vulnerable heels
will run away with them. . . .

" Mr. Lamborn refers to the late elections in
the States, and, from their results, confidently
predicts every State in the Union will vote for
Mr. Van Buren at the next presidential election.

Address that argument to cowards and knaves!
With the free and the brave it will effect nothing.
It may be true: if it must, let it. Many free
countries have lost their liberties, and ours may
lose hers; but if she shall, be it my proudest
plume, not that I was the last to desert, but that
I never deserted her. I know that the great
volcano at Washington, aroused and directed by
the evil spirit that reigns there, is belching forth
the lava of political corruption in a current broad
and deep, which is sweeping with frightful velocity
over the whole length and breadth of the land,
bidding fair to leave unscathed no green spot or
living thing, while on its bosom are riding, like
demons on the wave of hell, the imps of that evil
spirit, and fiendishly taunting all those who dare
to resist its destroying course with the hopeless-
ness of their efforts; and, knowing this, I cannot
deny that all may be swept away. Broken by it,
I too may be; bow to it, I never will. The
probability that we may fall in the struggle ought
not to deter us from the support of a cause we
believe to be just. It shall not deter me. If
ever I feel the soul within me elevate and expand
to those dimensions not wholly unworthy of its
Almighty Architect, it is when I contemplate the
cause of my country deserted by all the world

beside, and I standing up, boldly, alone, hurling
defiance at her victorious oppressors. Here, without contemplating consequences, before Heaven
and in the face of the world, I swear eternal
fealty to the just cause, as I deem it, of the land
of my life, my liberty, and my love. And who
that thinks with me will not fearlessly adopt the
oath that I take? Let none falter who thinks he
is right, and we may succeed. But if, after all,
we shall fail, be it so; we still shall have the
proud consolation of saying to our consciences
and to the departed shade of our country's freedom, that the cause approved of our judgment
and adored of our hearts, in disaster, in chains, in
torture, in death, we never faltered in defending."

EXTRACTS FROM HIS ADDRESS BEFORE THE SPRING-
FIELD WASHINGTONIAN TEMPERANCE SOCIETY.

February 22, 1842.

"ALTHOUGH the temperance cause has been
in progress for nearly twenty years, it is apparent
to all that it is just now being crowned with a
degree of success hitherto unparalleled.

"The list of its friends is daily swelled by the
additions of fifties, of hundreds, and of thousands.
The cause itself seems suddenly transformed from

a cold abstract theory to a living, breathing, active and powerful chieftain, going forth conquering and to conquer. The citadels of his great adversary are daily being stormed and dismantled; his temples and his altars, where the rites of his idolatrous worship have long been performed, and where human sacrifices have long been wont to be made, are daily desecrated and deserted. The trump of the conqueror's fame is sounding from hill to hill, from sea to sea, and from land to land, and calling millions to his standard at a blast.

.   .   .   .

" 'But,' say some, 'we are no drunkards, and we shall not acknowledge ourselves such by joining a reform drunkard's society, whatever our influence might be.' Surely no Christian will adhere to this objection.

" If they believe, as they profess, that Omnipotence condescended to take on himself the form of sinful man, and, as such, to die an ignominious death for their sakes, surely they will not refuse submission to the infinitely lesser condescension for the temporal and perhaps eternal salvation of a large, erring, and unfortunate class of their fellow-creatures; nor is the condescension very great. In my judgment, such of us as have

never fallen victims have been spared more from
the absence of appetite, than from any mental or
moral superiority over those who have. Indeed,
I believe if we take habitual drunkards as a class,
their heads and their hearts will bear an advantageous comparison with those of any other class.
There seems ever to have been a proneness in the
brilliant and warm-blooded to fall into this vice.
The demon of intemperance ever seems to have
delighted in sucking the blood of genius and
generosity. What one of us but can call to
mind some relative more promising in youth than
all his fellows, who has fallen a sacrifice to his
rapacity? He ever seems to have gone forth
like the Egyptian angel of death, commissioned
to slay, if not the first, the fairest born of every
family. Shall he now be arrested in his deso-
lating career? In that arrest all can give aid
that will; and who shall be excused that can and
will not? Far around as human breath has ever
blown, he keeps our fathers, our brothers, our
sons, and our friends prostrate in the chains of
moral death. To all the living everywhere we
cry, 'Come, sound the moral trump, that these
may rise and stand up an exceeding great army!'
'Come from the four winds, O breath, and
breathe upon these slain, that they may live!'

If the relative grandeur of revolutions shall be estimated by the great amount of human misery they alleviate, and the small amount they inflict, then, indeed, will this be the grandest the world shall ever have seen.

" Of our political revolution of '76, we are all justly proud. It has given us a degree of political freedom far exceeding that of any other nations of the earth. In it the world has found a solution of the long-mooted problem as to the capability of man to govern himself. In it was the germ which has vegetated, and still is to grow and expand into the universal liberty of mankind.

" But with all these glorious results, past, present, and to come, it had its evils too. It breathed forth famine, swam in blood, and rode in fire ; and long, long after, the orphans' cry and the widows' wail continued to break the sad silence that ensued. These were the price, the inevitable price, paid for the blessings it bought.

" Turn now to the temperance revolution. In it we shall find a stronger bondage broken, a viler slavery manumitted, and a greater tyrant deposed ; in it, more of want supplied, more disease healed, more sorrow assuaged. By it no orphans starving, no widows weeping. By it none wounded in feeling, none injured in interest ; even the dram-maker and dram-seller will have glided into other occupations so gradually as never to have felt the change, and will stand ready to join all others in the universal song of gladness. And what a noble ally this to the cause of political freedom! with such an aid its march cannot fail to be on and on, till every son of earth shall drink in rich fruition the sorrow-quenching draughts of perfect liberty. Happy day when, all appetites controlled, all poisons subdued, all matter subjected, mind, all-conquering mind, shall live and move, the monarch of the world! Glorious consummation! Hail, fall of fury! Reign of reason, all hail!

"And when the victory shall be complete, — when there shall be neither a slave nor a drunkard on the earth, — how proud the title of that *Land* which may truly claim to be the birthplace and the cradle of both those revolutions that shall have ended in that victory! How nobly distinguished that people who shall have planted and nurtured to maturity both the political and moral freedom of their species!

"This is the one hundred and tenth anniversary of the birthday of Washington. We are met to celebrate this day. Washington is the mightiest name of earth, — long since mightiest in the cause

3

of civil liberty, still mightiest in moral reformation. On that name no eulogy is expected. It cannot be. To add brightness to the sun, or glory to the name of Washington, is alike impossible. Let none attempt it. In solemn awe pronounce the name, and in its naked, deathless splendour leave it shining on."

FROM THE CIRCULAR OF THE WHIG COMMITTEE.[1]

March 4, 1843.

" . . . As an individual who undertakes to live by borrowing soon finds his original means devoured by interest, and next, no one left to borrow from, so must it be with a government.

" We repeat, then, that a tariff sufficient for revenue, or a direct tax, must soon be resorted to ; and, indeed, we believe this alternative is now denied by no one. But which system shall be adopted? Some of our opponents in theory admit the propriety of a tariff sufficient for revenue, but even they will not in practice vote for such a tariff ; while others boldly advocate direct

---

[1] This address, signed by Mr. Lincoln and two other members of the Whig Committee, was written by Mr. Lincoln, and was an effective exposition of his principles at the time.

taxation. Inasmuch, therefore, as some of them boldly advocate direct taxation, and all the rest — or so nearly all as to make exceptions needless — refuse to adopt the tariff, we think it is doing them no injustice to class them all as advocates of direct taxation. Indeed, we believe they are only delaying an open avowal of the system till they can assure themselves that the people will tolerate it. Let us, then, briefly compare the two systems. The tariff is the cheaper system, because the duties, being collected in large parcels, at a few commercial points, will require comparatively few officers in their collection ; while by the direct tax system the land must be literally covered with assessors and collectors, going forth like swarms of Egyptian locusts, devouring every blade of grass and other green thing. And again by the tariff system the whole revenue is paid by the consumers of foreign goods, and those chiefly the luxuries and not the necessaries of life. By this system, the man who contents himself to live upon the products of his own country pays nothing at all. And surely that country is extensive enough, and its products abundant and varied enough, to answer all the real wants of its people. In short, by this system the burden of revenue falls almost entirely on the wealthy and luxurious few, while the substantial and labouring many, who live at home and upon home products, go entirely free. By the direct tax system, none can escape. However strictly the citizen may exclude from his premises all foreign luxuries, fine cloths, fine silks, rich wines, golden chains, and diamond rings, — still, for the possession of his house, his barn, and his homespun he is to be perpetually haunted and harassed by the tax-gatherer. With these views, we leave it to be determined whether we or our opponents are more truly democratic on the subject.

" . . . We declare it to be our solemn conviction that the Whigs are always a majority of this nation; and that to make them always successful needs but to get them all to the polls and to vote unitedly. This is the great desideratum. Let us make every effort to attain it. At every election, let every Whig act as though he knew the result to depend upon his action. In the great contest of 1840, some more than twenty-one hundred thousand votes were cast, and so surely as there shall be that many, with the ordinary increase added, cast in 1844, that surely will a Whig be elected President of the United States."

FROM HIS SPEECH IN THE HOUSE OF REPRESEN-
TATIVES OF THE UNITED STATES.[1]

July 27, 1848.

" . . . I have said General Taylor's position
is as well defined as is that of General Cass.
In saying this, I admit I do not certainly know
what he would do on the Wilmot proviso. I am
a Northern man, or rather a Western free-state
man, with a constituency I believe to be, and
with personal feelings I know to be, against the
extension of slavery. As such, and with what information I have, I hope and *believe* General Taylor, if elected, would not veto the proviso. But I
do not *know it.* Yet if I knew he would, I still

---

[1] No apology is deemed necessary for these selections
from Mr. Lincoln's last important speech in Congress. It
may be conceded that they are undignified; and yet they
indicate that the seed sown in his early life had not fallen
upon barren ground. It germinates slightly in his
eulogy upon Henry Clay, in 1852; it grows strong in the
speech at Peoria, in 1854; is still more vigorous in the
criticism of the Dred Scott decision, in 1857; and its rip-
ened fruit appears in the "Divided House" speech of
June, 1858. The speech of July 27, 1848, marks the end
of a stage in the intellectual growth of its author, — the
change of the politician into the statesman. It was the
time when he laid aside satire and ridicule, and thenceforward only made use of argument and historical or phi-
losophic demonstration.

would vote for him. I should do so, because, in my judgment, his election alone can defeat General Cass; and because, should slavery thereby go to the territory we now have, just so much will certainly happen by the election of Cass, and, in addition, a course of policy leading to new wars, new acquisitions of territory, and still further extensions of slavery. One of the two is to be President; which is preferable?

" . . . The other day, one of the gentlemen from Georgia [Mr. Iverson], an eloquent man, and a man of learning, so far as I can judge, not being learned myself, came down upon us astonishingly. He spoke in what the Baltimore 'American' calls ' the scathing and withering style.' At the end of his second severe flash I was struck blind, and found myself feeling with my fingers for an assurance of my continued physical existence. A little of the bone was left, and I gradually revived. He eulogised Mr. Clay in high and beautiful terms, and then declared that we had deserted all our principles, and had turned Henry Clay out, like an old horse, to root. This is terribly severe. It cannot be answered by argument; at least, I cannot so answer it. I merely wish to ask the gentleman if the Whigs are the only party he can think of who sometimes turn old

horses out to root.   Is not a certain Martin Van
Buren an old horse which your own party have
turned out to root? And is he not rooting to
your discomfort about now?

" . . . But the gentleman from Georgia further says we have deserted all our principles and
taken shelter under General Taylor's military
coat-tail, and he seems to think this is exceeding degrading.   Well, as his faith is, so be it unto
him.   But can he remember no other military
coat-tail under which a certain other party have
been sheltering for near a quarter of a century?
Has he no acquaintance with the ample military
coat-tail of General Jackson? Does he not know
that his own party have run the last five presidential races under that coat-tail, and that they
are now running the sixth under that same cover?
Yes, sir.   That coat-tail was used not only for
General Jackson himself, but has been clung to
with the grip of death by every Democratic candidate since.

" . . . By the way, Mr. Speaker, did you
know I am a military hero? Yes, sir, in the days
of the Black Hawk War, I fought, bled, and came
away.   Speaking of General Cass's career, reminds me of my own.   I was not at Stillman's
defeat, but I was about as near it as Cass was to

Hull's surrender; and, like him, I saw the place very soon afterward. It is quite certain I did not break my sword, for I had none to break; but I bent a musket pretty badly on one occasion. If Cass broke his sword, the idea is he broke it in desperation; I bent the musket by accident. If General Cass went in advance of me in picking huckleberries, I guess I surpassed him in charges upon the wild onions. If he saw any live fighting Indians, it was more than I did; but I had a good many bloody struggles with the mosquitoes, and although I never fainted from loss of blood, I can truly say I was often very hungry. . . ."

THE EULOGY UPON HENRY CLAY.

July 16, 1852.

NOTE. — The fact is mentioned by all the biographers of Mr. Lincoln, except Nicolay and Hay, that on the 16th of July, 1852, at the request of his fellow-citizens, he delivered, at the State House in Springfield, an eulogy upon Henry Clay. In the most comprehensive of these biographies, no mention appears to be made of this eulogy, and of at least one other address made by Mr. Lincoln. No selections are made from this eulogy for obvious reasons.

It was regarded at the time as unworthy of its writer. Dr. Holland says, "The eulogy was pronounced in the State House, and was listened to by a large audience. The discourse, as it was printed in the city newspapers of the day, was by no means a remarkable one. It is remembered as a very dull one at its delivery, and was so regarded by Mr. Lincoln himself, who complained that he lacked the imagination necessary for a performance of that character."

Mr. Lamon says, "Such addresses are usually called orations; but this one scarcely deserved the name. He made no effort to be eloquent, and in no part of it was he more than ordinarily animated. It is true that he bestowed great praise upon Mr. Clay; but it was bestowed in cold phrases and a tame style, wholly unlike the bulk of his previous compositions. . . . If the address upon Clay is of any historical value at all, it is because it discloses Mr. Lincoln's unreserved agreement with Mr. Clay in his opinions concerning slavery and the proper method of extinguishing it. They both favoured gradual emancipation by the voluntary action of the people of the slave States and the transportation of the whole negro population to Africa," etc.

Lapse of time and the distinguished career of its author have only served to confirm the justice of the contemporary criticisms of this paper. As it appears in the "Collected Writings" of its author, it is the most conspicuous of the two or three papers which do not illustrate the thoughtful preparation which Mr. Lincoln usually gave to his addresses, to which our literature is indebted for so many gems of thought which will permanently enrich and adorn its pages.

After a dry enumeration of the public offices filled by Mr. Clay, the eulogy includes a long obituary notice from one of the public journals, the name of which is not given. It mentions the public questions, including the Compromise of 1820, in which Mr. Clay took a leading part, and its remaining pages are occupied by an account of Mr. Clay's labours, in connection with the American Colonisation Society, in attempting to popularise the impossible scheme of abolishing slavery by the deportation of the negro race to Africa. One point in the eulogy is of some interest in view of the use afterwards made of it by Mr. Lincoln. It is his contention that the " Fathers " intended to include the negro in the statement in the Declaration of Independence, that " all men are created equal," and that Mr. Calhoun was the first American of any note to assail or ridicule the claim of the black man to a place in the " white man's charter of freedom." His comment upon Mr. Calhoun's new exposition has in it a spark of the Lincoln humour, and has a singular appropriateness in 1895. " We, however, look for and are not much shocked by political eccentricities and heresies in South Carolina."

There is not value enough in its few bright thoughts to relieve the dulness of this document.

No selections from it which would increase his fame or serve any useful purpose, are possible. It is omitted, then, with the consolatory reflection " *aliquando dormitat bonus Homerus.*"

FROM HIS REPLY TO SENATOR DOUGLAS, DELIVERED AT PEORIA, ILLINOIS. ORIGIN OF THE WILMOT PROVISO.[1]

October 16, 1854.

" . . . Our war with Mexico broke out in 1846. When Congress was about adjourning that session, President Polk asked them to place two millions of dollars under his control, to be used by him in the recess, if found practicable and expedient, in negotiating a treaty of peace with Mexico, and acquiring some part of her territory. A bill was duly gotten up for the purpose, and was progressing swimmingly in the House of Representatives, when a Democratic member from Pennsylvania by the name of David Wilmot moved as an amendment, ' Provided, that in any terri-

[1] This speech was written out by Mr. Lincoln, and published under his direction. It was his first speech which attracted public attention. It is important, because it shows the gradual growth of the argument presented in the "divided House" speech of June, 1858.

tory thus acquired there shall never be slavery.' *This is the origin of the far-famed Wilmot Proviso.* It created a great flutter; but it stuck like wax, was voted into the bill, and the bill passed with it through the House. The Senate, however, adjourned without final action on it, and so both the appropriation and the proviso were lost for the time.

" . . . This declared indifference, but, as I must think, real, covert zeal, for the spread of slavery, I cannot but hate. I hate it because of the monstrous injustice of slavery itself. I hate it because it deprives our republican example of its just influence in the world, enables the enemies of free institutions with plausibility to taunt us as hypocrites, causes the real friends of freedom to doubt our sincerity, and especially because it forces so many good men amongst ourselves into an open war with the very fundamental principles of civil liberty, criticising the Declaration of Independence, and insisting that there is no right principle of action but self-interest. . . .

" . . . Equal justice to the South, it is said, requires us to consent to the extension of slavery to new countries. That is to say, that inasmuch as you do not object to my taking my hog to Nebraska, therefore I must not object to your taking your slave. Now, I admit that this is perfectly logical, if there is no difference between hogs and slaves. But while you thus require me to deny the humanity of the negro, I wish to ask whether you of the South, yourselves, have ever been willing to do as much? It is kindly provided that of all those who come into the world, only a small percentage are natural tyrants. That percentage is no larger in the slave States than in the free. The great majority, South as well as North, have human sympathies, of which they can no more divest themselves than they can of their sensibility to physical pain. These sympathies in the bosoms of the Southern people manifest in many ways their sense of the wrong of slavery, and their consciousness that, after all, there is humanity in the negro. . . . In 1820 you joined the North almost unanimously in declaring the African slave-trade piracy, and in annexing to it the punishment of death. Why did you do this? If you did not feel that it was wrong, why did you join in providing that men should be hung for it? The practice was no more than bringing wild negroes from Africa to such as would buy them. But you never thought of hanging men for catching and selling wild horses, wild buffaloes, or wild bears.

" Again, you have among you a sneaking indi-vidual of the class of native tyrants known as the *slave-dealer*. He watches your necessities, and crawls up to buy your slave at a speculating price. If you cannot help it, you sell to him; but if you can help it, you drive him from your door. You despise him utterly; you do not recognise him as a friend, or even as an honest man. Your children must not play with his; they may rollick freely with the little negroes, but not with the slave-dealer's children. If you are obliged to deal with him, you try to get through the job without so much as touching him. It is common with you to join hands with the men you meet; but with the slave-dealer you avoid the ceremony, — instinctively shrinking from the snaky contact. If he grows rich and retires from business, you still remember him, and still keep up the ban of non-intercourse upon him and his family. Now, why is this?

" . . . And yet again. There are in the United States and Territories, including the Dis-trict of Columbia, over four hundred and thirty thousand free blacks. At five hundred dollars per head, they are worth over two hundred mil-lions of dollars. How comes this vast amount of property to be running about without owners?

We do not see free horses or free cattle running
at large. How is this? All these free blacks are
the descendants of slaves, or have been slaves
themselves; and they would be slaves now but
for something which has operated on their white
owners, inducing them at vast pecuniary sacrifice
to liberate them. What is that something? Is
there any mistaking it? In all these cases it is
your sense of justice and human sympathy continually telling you that the poor negro has some
natural right to himself, — that those who deny it
and make mere merchandise of him deserve kick-
ings, contempt, and death.

" . . . But one great argument in support of
the repeal of the Missouri Compromise is still to
come. That argument is 'the sacred right of
self-government.' . . . Some poet has said, —

'Fools rush in where angels fear to tread.'

At the hazard of being thought one of the fools
of this quotation, I meet that argument, — I rush
in, — I take that bull by the horns. . . . My
faith in the proposition that each man should do
precisely as he pleases with all which is exclusively his own, lies at the foundation of the sense
of justice there is in me. I extend the principle to communities of men as well as to indi-

viduals. I so extend it because it is politically wise as well as naturally just, — politically wise in saving us from broils about matters which do not concern us. Here, or at Washington, I would not trouble myself with the oyster laws of Virginia, or the cranberry laws of Indiana. The doctrine of self-government is right, — absolutely and eternally right; but it has no just application as here attempted. Or perhaps I should rather say that whether it has any application here depends upon whether a negro is not or is a man. If he is not a man, in that case he who is a man may, as a matter of self-government, do just what he pleases with him. But if the negro is a man, is it not to that extent a total destruction of self-government to say that he, too, shall not govern himself? When the white man governs himself, that is self-government; but when he governs himself and also governs another man, that is more than self-government, — that is despotism. If the negro is a man, then my ancient faith teaches me that 'all men are created equal,' and that there can be no moral right in connection with one man's making a slave of another.

" . . . Frequently and with bitter irony our argument is paraphrased by saying, 'The white people of Nebraska are good enough to govern

themselves, but they are not good enough to govern a few miserable negroes!'

" Well, I doubt not that the people of Nebraska are and will continue to be as good as
the average of people elsewhere. I do not say
the contrary. What I do say is that no man is
good enough to govern another man without
that other's consent. I say this is the leading principle, — the sheet-anchor of American
republicanism.

" . . . Slavery is founded in the selfishness of
man's nature, — opposition to it in his love of justice. These principles are in eternal antagonism,
and when brought into collision so fiercely as slavery extension brings them, shocks and throes and
convulsions must ceaselessly follow. Repeal the
Missouri Compromise ; repeal all compromises ;
repeal the Declaration of Independence ; repeal
all past history, — you still cannot repeal human
nature. It still will be the abundance of man's
heart that slavery extension is wrong, and out of
the abundance of his heart his mouth will continue to speak. . . .

" The Missouri Compromise ought to be restored. . . . But whether it be or not, we shall
have repudiated — discarded from the councils
of the nation — the spirit of compromise ;

for who, after this, will ever trust in a national compromise? The spirit of mutual concession — that spirit which first gave us the Constitution, and has thrice saved the Union — we shall have strangled and cast from us for ever. And what shall we have in lieu of it? The South flushed with triumph and tempted to excess; the North betrayed, as they believe, brooding on wrong and burning for revenge. One side will provoke, the other resent. The one will taunt, the other defy; one aggresses, the other retaliates. Already a few in the North defy all constitutional restraints, resist the execution of the Fugitive Slave Law, and even menace the institution of slavery in the States where it exists. Already a few in the South claim the constitutional right to take and hold slaves in the free States, demand the revival of the slave-trade, and demand a treaty with Great Britain by which fugitive slaves may be reclaimed from Canada. As yet they are but few on either side. It is a grave question for lovers of the Union, whether the final destruction of the Missouri Compromise, and with it the spirit of all compromise, will or will not embolden and embitter each of these, and fatally increase the number of both.

" . . . Some men, mostly Whigs, who con- demn the repeal of the Missouri Compromise, nevertheless hesitate to go for its restoration, lest they be thrown in company with the Abolitionists. Will they allow me, as an old Whig, to tell them good-humouredly that I think this is very silly? Stand with anybody that stands right. Stand with him while he is right, and part with him when he goes wrong. Stand with the Abolitionist in restoring the Missouri Compromise, and stand against him when he attempts to repeal the Fugitive Slave Law. . . . In both cases you are right. . . . In both you are national, and nothing less than national. . . . To desert such ground because of any company is to be less than a Whig, less than a man, less than an American.

" I particularly object to the new position which the avowed principle of this Nebraska law gives to slavery in the body politic. I object to it because it assumes that there can be moral right in the enslaving of one man by another. . . . I object to it because the Fathers of the Republic eschewed and rejected it. . . . The plain, unmistakable spirit of their age towards slavery was hostility to the principle, and toleration only by necessity.

" But now it is to be transformed into a *sacred right*. . . . Henceforth it is to be the chief jewel of the nation, — the very figure-head of the ship of State. Little by little, but steadily as man's march to the grave, we have been giving up the old for the new faith. Near eighty years ago we began by declaring that all men are created equal; but now from that beginning we have run down to the other declaration, that for some men to enslave others is a sacred right of self-government. These principles cannot stand together. They are as opposite as God and Mammon; and whoever holds to the one must despise the other. . . .

" Our Republican robe is soiled and trailed in the dust. Let us purify it. Let us turn and wash it white in the spirit if not the blood of the Revolution. Let us turn slavery from its claims of moral right, back upon its existing legal rights and its arguments of necessity. Let us return it to the position our fathers gave it, and there let it rest in peace. Let us re-adopt the Declaration of Independence, and with it the practices and policy which harmonise with it. Let North and South, let all Americans, let all lovers of liberty everywhere, join in the great and good work. If we do this, we shall not only have saved the Union, but we shall have so saved it as to make and to keep it for ever worthy of the saving.

We shall have so saved it that the succeeding millions of free, happy people, the world over, shall rise up and call us blessed to the latest generations. . . ."

EXTRACTS FROM LETTER TO JOSHUA F. SPEED.[1]

August 24, 1855.

" . . . You suggest that in political action now, you and I would differ. I suppose we would; not quite so much, however, as you may think. You know I dislike slavery, and you fully admit the abstract wrong of it. So far there is no cause of difference. But you say that sooner than yield your legal right to the slave, especially at the bidding of those who are not themselves interested, you would see the Union dissolved. I am not aware that any one is bidding you yield that right; very certainly I am not. I leave that matter entirely to yourself. I also acknowledge your rights and my obligations under the Consti-

---

[1] In this letter to his intimate friend, as a justification of his dislike of slavery, Mr. Lincoln is supposed to have referred to his first object-lesson of the evils of the institution. If the incident of the slave auction in New Orleans had occurred, it is believed that he would have referred to it in this letter, which is a beautiful illustration of the sincerity of its author.

tution in regard to your slaves. I confess I hate to see the poor creatures hunted down and caught and carried back to their stripes and unrequited toil; but I bite my lips and keep quiet. In 1841, you and I had together a tedious low-water trip on a steamboat, from Louisville to St. Louis. You may remember, as I well do, that from Louisville to the mouth of the Ohio, there were on board ten or a dozen slaves shackled together with irons. That sight was a continued torment to me, and I see something like it every time I touch the Ohio or any other slave border. It is not fair for you to assume that I have no interest in a thing which has, and continually exercises, the power of making me miserable. You ought rather to appreciate how much the great body of the Northern people do crucify their feelings in order to maintain their loyalty to the Constitution and the Union. I do oppose the extension of slavery, because my judgment and feeling so prompt me, and I am under no obligations to the contrary. If for this you and I must differ, differ we must. You say if you were President, you would send an army and hang the leaders of the Missouri outrages upon the Kansas elections; still, if Kansas fairly votes herself a slave State she must be admitted, or the Union must be dissolved. But how if she votes herself a slave State unfairly ; that is, by the very means for which you say you would hang men? Must she still be admitted, or the Union dissolved? That will be the phase of the question when it first becomes a practical one. In your assumption that there may be a fair decision of the slavery question in Kansas, I plainly see that you and I would differ about the Nebraska law. I look upon that enactment, not as a law, but as a violence from the beginning. It was conceived in violence, is maintained in violence, and is being executed in violence. I say it was conceived in violence, because the destruction of the Missouri Compromise, under the circumstances, was nothing less than violence. It was passed in violence, because it could not have passed at all but for the votes of many members in violence of the known will of their constituents. It is maintained in violence, because the elections since clearly demand its repeal, and the demand is openly disregarded.

"You say men ought to be hung for the way they are executing the law ; I say that the way it is being executed is quite as good as any of its antecedents. It is being executed in the precise way which was intended from the first, else why does no Nebraska man express astonishment or condemnation? Poor Reeder is the only public man who has been silly enough to believe that anything like fairness was ever intended, and he has been bravely undeceived.

"That Kansas will form a slave constitution, and with it ask to be admitted into the Union, I take to be already a settled question, and so settled by the very means you so pointedly condemn. By every principle of law ever held by any court North or South, every negro taken to Kansas is free; yet in utter disregard of this — in the spirit of violence merely — that beautiful Legislature gravely passes a law to hang any man who shall venture to inform a negro of his legal rights. This is the subject and real object of the law. If, like Haman, they should hang upon the gallows of their own building, I shall not be among the mourners for their fate. In my humble sphere, I shall advocate the restoration of the Missouri Compromise so long as Kansas remains a Territory; and when, by all these foul means, it seeks to come into the Union as a slave State, I shall oppose it. I am very loath in any case to withhold my assent to the enjoyment of property acquired or located in good faith; but I do not admit that good faith in taking a negro to Kansas to be held in slavery

is a probability with any man. Any man who
has sense enough to be the controller of his own
property has too much sense to misunderstand
the outrageous character of the whole Nebraska
business. But I digress. In my opposition to
the admission of Kansas, I shall have some company, but we may be beaten. If we are, I shall
not, on that account, attempt to dissolve the
Union. I think it probable, however, we shall
be beaten. Standing as a unit among yourselves,
you can, directly and indirectly, bribe enough of
our men to carry the day, as you could on the
open proposition to establish a monarchy. Get
hold of some man in the North whose position
and ability are such that he can make the support of your measure, whatever it may be, a
Democratic-party necessity, and the thing is
done. Apropos of this, let me tell you an anec-
dote. Douglas introduced the Nebraska Bill in
January. In February afterward, there was a
called session of the Illinois Legislature. Of
the one hundred members composing the two
branches of that body, about seventy were Democrats. These latter held a caucus, in which the
Nebraska Bill was talked of, if not formally discussed. It was thereby discovered that just three,
and no more, were in favour of the measure. In

a day or two Douglas's orders came on to have
resolutions passed approving the bill; and they
were passed by large majorities! The truth of
this is vouched for by a bolting Democratic
member. The masses too, Democratic as well
as Whig, were even nearer unanimous against it;
but as soon as the party necessity of supporting
it became apparent, the way the Democrats began to see the wisdom and justice of it was
perfectly astonishing.

" You say that if Kansas fairly votes herself a
free State, as a Christian you will rejoice at it.
All decent slaveholders talk that way, and I do
not doubt their candour; but they never vote
that way. Although in a private letter or conversation you will express your preference that
Kansas should be free, you would vote for no
man for Congress who would say the same thing
publicly. No such man could be elected from
any district in a slave State. You think String-
fellow and company ought to be hung. . . .
The slave-breeders and slave-traders are a small,
odious, and detested class among you; and yet
in politics they dictate the course of all of you,
and are as completely your masters as you are
the master of your own negroes. You inquire
where I now stand. That is a disputed point.

I think I am a Whig; but others say there are
no Whigs, and that I am an Abolitionist. When
I was at Washington, I voted for the Wilmot Proviso as good as forty times; and I never heard
of any one attempting to unwhig me for that.
I now do no more than oppose the extension of
slavery. I am not a Know-nothing; that is certain. How could I be? How can any one who
abhors the oppression of negroes be in favour
of degrading classes of white people? Our
progress in degeneracy appears to me to be
pretty rapid. As a nation, we began by declaring
that *all men are created equal.* We now practically read it, *all men are created equal except
negroes.* When the Know-nothings get control,
it will read, *all men are created equal except negroes* and foreigners and Catholics. When it
comes to this, I shall prefer emigrating to some
country where they make no pretence of loving
liberty — to Russia, for instance, where despotism can be taken pure, and without the base
alloy of hypocrisy. . . ."

June 26, 1857.

" . . . And now as to the Dred Scott decision. That decision declares two propositions, — first, that a negro cannot sue in the United States courts ; and secondly, that Congress cannot prohibit slavery in the Territories. It was made by a divided court, — dividing differently on the different points. Judge Douglas does not discuss the merits of the decision, and in that respect I shall follow his example, believing I

---

[1] The biographers of Mr. Lincoln do not seem to have given to this speech the credit to which it is entitled. One of them says, it was "not of much consequence." No doubt it would have attracted more notice had Mr. Lincoln been better known ; but when it is remembered that the speech was delivered within six months after the Dred Scott decision was made ; that it pointed out the far-reaching force of that decision ; that it opened all the territories to slavery against the will of the people and the territorial legislature ; that it was a masterly analysis of the views of the majority of the court, and did not touch the right of the people to labour for its reversal, — this speech will be found worthy of its place in history, following the speech at Peoria, the letter to Mr. Speed, and to be followed by the "divided House" speech of the next year.

could no more improve on McLean and Curtis than he could on Taney.

"He denounces all who question the correctness of that decision, as offering violent resistance to it. But who resists it? Who has, in spite of the decision, declared Dred Scott free, and resisted the authority of his master over him?

"Judicial decisions have two uses: first, to absolutely determine the case decided; and secondly, to indicate to the public how other similar cases will be decided when they arise. For the latter use, they are called 'precedents' and 'authorities.'

"We believe as much as Judge Douglas (perhaps more) in obedience to and respect for the judicial department of government. We think its decisions on constitutional questions, when fully settled, should control not only the particular cases decided, but the general policy of the country, subject to be disturbed only by amendments of the Constitution, as provided in that instrument itself. More than this would be revolution. But we think the Dred Scott decision is erroneous. We know the court that made it has often overruled its own decisions, and we shall do what we can to have it overrule this. We offer no resistance to it.

" Judicial decisions are of greater or less authority as precedents according to circumstances. That this should be so, accords both with common-sense and the customary understanding of the legal profession.

" If this important decision had been made by the unanimous concurrence of the judges, and without any apparent partisan bias, and in accordance with legal public expectation, and with the steady practice of the departments throughout our history, and had been in no part based on assumed historical facts, which are not really true ; or if wanting in some of these, it had been before the court more than once, and had there been affirmed and reaffirmed through a course of years, — it then might be, perhaps would be factious, nay, even revolutionary, not to acquiesce in it as a precedent.

" But when, as is true, we find it wanting in all these claims to the public confidence, it is not resistance, it is not factious, it is not even disrespectful to treat it as not having yet quite established a settled doctrine for the country.

" . . . The Chief Justice does not directly assert, but plainly assumes as a fact, that the public estimate of the black man is more favourable now than it was in the days of the Revolution. This assumption is a mistake. In some trifling particulars the condition of that race has been ameliorated; but as a whole, in this country, the change between then and now is decidedly the other way; and their ultimate destiny has never appeared so hopeless as in the last three or four years. In two of the five States — New Jersey and North Carolina — that then gave the free negro the right of voting, the right has since been taken away; and in a third, New York, it has been greatly abridged: while it has not been extended, so far as I know, to a single additional State, though the number of the States has more than doubled. In those days, as I understand, masters could, at their own pleasure, emancipate their slaves; but since then such legal restraints have been made upon emancipation as to amount almost to prohibition. In those days legislatures held the unquestioned power to abolish slavery in their respective States; but now it is becoming quite fashionable for State constitutions to withhold that power from the legislatures. In those days, by common consent, the spread of the black man's bondage to the new countries was prohibited; but now Congress decides that it will not continue the prohibition, and the Supreme Court decides that it could not if it would. In those days our Declaration of Independence was held sacred by all, and thought to include all; but now, to aid in making the bondage of the negro universal and eternal, it is assailed and sneered at, and construed, and hawked at, and torn, till, if its framers could rise from their graves, they could not at all recognise it. All the powers of earth seem rapidly combining against him. Mammon is after him; ambition follows, philosophy follows, and the theology of the day is fast joining in the cry. They have him in his prison-house; they have searched his person, and left no prying instrument with him. One after another they have closed the heavy iron doors upon him; and now they have him, as it were, bolted in with a lock of a hundred keys, which can never be unlocked without the concurrence of every key; the keys in the hands of a hundred different men, and they scattered to a hundred different and distant places; and they stand musing as to what invention, in all the dominions of mind and matter, can be produced to make the impossibility of escape more complete than it is. It is grossly incorrect to say or assume that the public estimate of the negro is more favourable now than it was at the origin of the government.

" . . . There is a natural disgust in the minds of nearly all white people at the idea of an indiscriminate amalgamation of the white and black races; and Judge Douglas evidently is basing his chief hope upon the chances of his being able to appropriate the benefit of this disgust to himself. If he can, by much drumming and repeating, fasten the odium of that idea upon his adversaries, he thinks he can struggle through the storm. He therefore clings to this hope as a drowning man to the last plank. He makes an occasion for lugging it in from the opposition to the Dred Scott decision. He finds the Republicans insisting that the Declaration of Independence includes *all* men, black as well as white; and forthwith he boldly denies that it includes negroes at all, and proceeds to arguely gravely that all who contend it does, do so only because they want to vote, and eat, and sleep, and marry with negroes! He will have it that they cannot be consistent else. Now I protest against the counterfeit logic which concludes that because I do not want a black woman for a slave, I must necessarily want her for a wife. I need not have her for either. I can just leave her alone. In some respects she certainly is not my equal; but in her natural right to eat the

5

bread she earns with her own hands without asking leave of any one else, she is my equal, and the
equal of all others.

"Chief Justice Taney, in his opinion in the
Dred Scott case, admits that the language of the
Declaration is broad enough to include the whole
human family; but he and Judge Douglas argue
that the authors of that instrument did not intend to include negroes, by the fact that they did
not at once actually place them on an equality
with the whites.   Now this grave argument comes
to just nothing at all, by the other fact that they
did not at once, nor ever afterward, actually place
all white people on an equality with one another.
And this is the staple argument of both the Chief
Justice and the senator, for doing this obvious
violence to the plain, unmistakable language of
the Declaration.

"I think the authors of that notable instrument intended to include *all* men, but they did
not intend to declare all men equal *in all respects*.
They did not mean to say that all were equal in
color, size, intellect, moral developments, or social
capacity.   They defined with tolerable distinct-
ness in what respects they did consider all men
created equal, — equal with 'certain inalienable
rights, among which are life, liberty, and the pur-

suit of happiness.' This they said, and this they meant. They did not mean to assert the obvious untruth that all were then actually enjoying that equality, nor yet that they were about to confer it immediately upon them. In fact, they had no power to confer such a boon. They meant simply to declare the right, so that the enforcement of it might follow as fast as circumstances should permit.

"They meant to set up a standard maxim for free society, which should be familiar to all and revered by all, — constantly looked to, constantly laboured for, and, even though never perfectly attained, constantly approximated, and thereby constantly spreading and deepening its influence, and augmenting the happiness and value of life to all people of all colours everywhere. The assertion that 'all men are created equal,' was of no practical use in effecting our separation from Great Britain ; and it was placed in the Declaration, not for that, but for future use. Its authors meant it to be as, thank God, it is now proving itself, a stumbling-block to all those who in after times might seek to turn a free people back into the hateful paths of despotism. They knew the proneness of prosperity to breed tyrants, and they meant, when such should reappear in this fair land

and commence their vocation, that they should find left for them at least one hard nut to crack.

"... Judge Douglas makes a mere wreck, a mangled ruin, of our once glorious Declaration. He says ' they were speaking of British subjects on this continent being equal to British subjects born and residing in Great Britain!' Why, according to this, not only negroes but white people outside of Great Britain and America were not spoken of in that instrument. The English, Irish, and Scotch, along with white Americans, were included, to be sure; but the French, Germans, and other white people of the world are all gone to pot along with the Judge's inferior races!

"I had thought that the Declaration promised something better than the condition of British subjects; but no, it only meant that we should be equal to them in their own oppressed and unequal condition. According to that, it gave no promise that, having kicked off the king and lords of Great Britain, we should not at once be saddled with a king and lords of our own.

"I had thought the Declaration contemplated the progressive improvement in the condition of all men, everywhere; but no, it merely ' was adopted for the purpose of justifying the colonists in the eyes of the civilised world in withdrawing their allegiance from the British crown, and dissolving their connection with the mother-country.' Why, that object having been effected some eighty years ago, the Declaration is of no practical use now — mere rubbish — old wadding, left to rot on the battle-field after the victory is won.

" I understand you are preparing to celebrate the ' Fourth,' to-morrow week. What for? The doings of that day had no reference to the present ; and quite half of you are not even descendants of those who were referred to at that day. But I suppose you will celebrate, and will even go so far as to read the Declaration. Suppose, after you read it once in the old-fashioned way, you read it once more with Judge Douglas's version. It will then run thus : ' We hold these truths to be self-evident, that all British subjects who were on this continent eighty-one years ago, were created equal to all British subjects born and then residing in Great Britain !'

" . . . The very Dred Scott case affords a strong test as to which party most favours amalgamation, the Republicans or the dear Union-saving Democracy. Dred Scott, his wife and two daughters, were all involved in the suit. We desired the court to have held that they were citizens, so far at least as to entitle them to a hearing as to whether they were free or not ; and then also, that they were in fact and in law really free.   Could we have had our way, the chances of these black girls ever mixing their blood with that of white people would have been diminished at least to the extent that it could not have been without their consent.   But Judge Douglas is delighted to have them decided to be slaves, and not human enough to have a hearing, even if they were free, and thus left subject to the forced concubinage of their masters, and liable to become the mothers of mulattoes in spite of themselves, — the very state of the case that produces nine-tenths of all the mulattoes, all the mixing of the blood of the nation.

" . . . Let us be brought to believe it is morally right, and at the same time favourable to, or at least not against our interest to transfer the African to his native clime, and we shall find a way to do it, however great the task may be.   The children of Israel, to such numbers as to include four hundred thousand fighting men, went out of Egyptian bondage in a body.

" . . . The plainest print cannot be read through a gold eagle ; and it will be ever hard to find many men who will send a slave to Li-

beria and pay his passage, while they can send
him to a new country — Kansas, for instance —
and sell him for fifteen hundred dollars and the
rise."

THE "DIVIDED HOUSE" SPEECH DELIVERED AT
SPRINGFIELD, ILLINOIS, ON HIS NOMINATION TO
THE SENATE OF THE UNITED STATES.[1]

June 17, 1858.

IF we could first know where we are, and
whither we are tending, we could better judge
what to do, and how to do it. We are now far
into the fifth year since a policy was initiated

---

[1] This speech is the most important ever made by Mr.
Lincoln. It was printed and circulated with the report
of the Lincoln and Douglas debate, and it brought its
author prominently before the people of the whole country. No careful reader of this speech will fail to discover
that it cannot be condensed, that no paragraph in it can
be omitted without weakening its logic, injuring its style,
and doing injustice to its author. It has an interesting
history which it does not fall within the scope of this volume to give. It should always be presented in its en-
tirety, to maintain its own position as a model for political
speakers, a specimen of English composition, and, whether
judged by its intrinsic qualities or its influence upon the
fortunes of the Republic, one of the greatest of all political documents since the Declaration of Independence.

with the avowed object and confident promise of putting an end to slavery agitation. Under the operation of that policy, that agitation has not only not ceased, but has constantly augmented. In my opinion it will not cease until a crisis shall have been reached and passed. "A house divided against itself cannot stand." I believe this government cannot endure permanently, half slave and half free. I do not expect the Union to be dissolved, — I do not expect the house to fall; but I do expect it will cease to be divided. It will become all one thing, or all the other. Either the opponents of slavery will arrest the further spread of it, and place it where the public mind shall rest in the belief that it is in the course of ultimate extinction; or its advocates will push it forward till it shall become alike lawful in all the States, old as well as new, North as well as South.

Have we no tendency to the latter condition? Let any one who doubts, carefully contemplate that now almost complete legal combination — piece of machinery, so to speak — compounded of the Nebraska doctrine and the Dred Scott decision. Let him consider not only what work the machinery is adapted to do, and how well adapted; but also let him study the history of its construction, and trace, if he can, or rather fail, if he can, to trace the evidences of design and concert of action among its chief architects from the beginning.

The new year of 1854 found slavery excluded from more than half the States by State constitutions, and from most of the national territory by congressional prohibition. Four days later commenced the struggle which ended in repealing that congressional prohibition. This opened all the national territory to slavery, and was the first point gained.

But so far, Congress only had acted; and an indorsement by the people, real or apparent, was indispensable to save the point already gained and give chance for more.

This necessity had not been overlooked, but had been provided for, as well as might be, in the notable argument of *Squatter Sovereignty*, otherwise called *sacred right of self-government*, which latter phrase, though expressive of the only rightful basis of any government, was so perverted in this attempted use of it, as to amount to just this: That if any one man choose to enslave another, no third man shall be allowed to object. That argument was incorporated into the Nebraska Bill itself, in the language which follows: " It being the true intent and meaning of this act, not to legislate slavery into any Territory or State, nor to exclude it therefrom ; but to leave the people thereof perfectly free to form and regulate their domestic institutions in their own way, subject only to the Constitution of the United States." Then opened the roar of loose declamation in favour of *Squatter Sovereignty* and *sacred right of self-government.* " But," said opposition members, " let us amend the bill so as to expressly declare that the people of the Territory may exclude slavery." " Not we," said the friends of the measure, and down they voted the amendment.

While the Nebraska Bill was passing through Congress, a *law case,* involving the question of a negro's freedom, by reason of his owner having voluntarily taken him first into a free State and then into a Territory covered by the congressional prohibition, and held him as a slave for a long time in each, was passing through the United States Circuit Court for the District of Missouri ; and both Nebraska Bill and lawsuit were brought to a decision, in the same month of May, 1854. The negro's name was " Dred Scott," which name now designates the decision finally rendered in the case. Before the then

next presidential election, the law case came to, and was argued, in the Supreme Court of the United States ; but the decision of it was deferred until after the election. Still, before the election, Senator Trumbull, on the floor of the Senate, requested the leading advocate of the Nebraska Bill to state *his opinion* whether the people of a Territory can constitutionally exclude slavery from their limits, and the latter answers : "That is a question for the Supreme Court."

The election came. Mr. Buchanan was elected, and the indorsement, such as it was, secured. That was the second point gained. The indorsement, however, fell short of a clear popular majority by nearly four hundred thousand votes, and so, perhaps, was not overwhelmingly reliable and satisfactory. The outgoing President, in his last annual message, as impressively as possible echoed back upon the people the weight and authority of the indorsement. The Supreme Court met again ; did not announce their decision, but ordered a reargument. The presidential inauguration came, and still no decision of the Court ; but the incoming President in his inaugural address fervently exhorted the people to abide by the forthcoming decision, whatever it might be. Then, in a few days, came the decision.

The reputed author of the Nebraska Bill finds an early occasion to make a speech at this capitol, indorsing the Dred Scott decision, and vehemently denouncing all opposition to it. The new President, too, seizes the early occasion of the Silliman letter to indorse and strongly construe that decision, and to express his astonishment that any different view had ever been entertained !

At length a squabble springs up between the President and the author of the Nebraska Bill, on the mere question of *fact* whether the Lecompton constitution was, or was not, in any just sense, made by the people of Kansas ; and in that quarrel, the latter declares that all he wants is a fair vote for the people, and that he cares not whether slavery be voted *down* or *voted up*. I do not understand his declaration that he cares not whether slavery be voted down or voted up, to be intended by him other than as an apt definition of the policy he would impress upon the public mind, — the principle for which he declares he has suffered so much, and is ready to suffer to the end. And well may he cling to that principle. If he has any parental feeling, well may he cling to it. That principle is the only shred left of his original Nebraska doctrine. Under the Dred Scott decision, "squatter sovereignty"

squatted out of existence, tumbled down like
temporary scaffolding; like the mould at the
foundry, it served through one blast, and fell back
into loose sand,—helped to carry an election,
and then was kicked to the winds. His late joint
struggle with the Republicans against the Lecompton constitution, involves nothing of the
original Nebraska doctrine. That struggle was
made on a point — the right of the people to
make their own constitution — upon which he
and the Republicans have never differed.

The several points of the Dred Scott decision
in connection with Senator Douglas's "care not"
policy, constitute the piece of machinery in its
present state of advancement. This was the
third point gained. The working points of that
machinery are : —

First. That no negro slave, imported as such
from Africa, and no descendant of such slave,
can ever be a citizen of any State, in the sense of
that term as used in the Constitution of the United
States. This point is made in order to deprive
the negro, in every possible event, of the benefit
of that provision of the United States Constitution which declares that "citizens of each State
shall be entitled to all privileges and immunities
of citizens in the several States."

Secondly. That " subject to the Constitution of the United States," neither Congress nor a territorial legislature can exclude slavery from any United States Territory. This point is made in order that individual men may fill up the Territories with slaves, without danger of losing them as property, and thus enhance the chances of permanency to the institution through all the future.

Thirdly. That whether the holding a negro in actual slavery in a free State makes him free as against the holder, the United States Courts will not decide, but will leave to be decided by the courts of any slave State the negro may be forced into by the master. This point is made, not to be pressed immediately ; but if acquiesced in for a while, and apparently indorsed by the people at an election, then to sustain the logical conclusion that what Dred Scott's master might lawfully do with Dred Scott in the free State of Illinois, every other master may lawfully do, with any other one, or one thousand slaves in Illinois, or in any other free State.

Auxiliary to all this, and working hand in hand with it, the Nebraska doctrine, or what is left of it, is to educate and mould public opinion not to care whether slavery is voted down or voted up.

This shows exactly where we now are, and partially, also, whither we are tending.

It will throw additional light on the latter, to go back, and run the mind over the string of historical facts already stated. Several things will now appear less dark and mysterious than they did when they were transpiring. The people were to be left "perfectly free," "subject only to the Constitution." What the Constitution had to do with it, outsiders could not then see. Plainly enough now; it was an exactly fitted niche for the Dred Scott decision to afterwards come in, and declare the perfect freedom of the people to be just no freedom at all. Why was the amendment expressly declaring the right of the people voted down? Plainly enough now: the adoption of it would have spoiled the niche for the Dred Scott decision. Why was the Court decision held up? Why even a Senator's individual opinion withheld till after the presidential election? Plainly enough now: the speaking out then would have damaged the perfectly free argument upon which the election was to be carried. Why the outgoing President's felicitation on the indorsement? Why the delay of a reargument? Why the incoming President's advance exhortation in favour of the decision? These things look like the cautious patting and petting of a spirited horse, preparatory to mounting him, when it is dreaded that he may give the rider a fall.   And why the hasty after-indorsement of the decision by the President and others?

We cannot absolutely know that all these adaptations are the result of preconcert.   But when we see a lot of framed timbers, different portions of which we know have been gotten out at different times and places, and by different workmen — Stephen, Franklin, Roger, and James, for instance (Douglas, Pierce, Taney, Buchanan), — and when we see those timbers joined together, and see they exactly make the frame of a house or a mill, all the tenons and mortices exactly fitting, and all the lengths and proportions of the different pieces exactly adapted to their respective places, and not a piece too many or too few, not omitting even scaffolding — or if a single piece be lacking, we see the place in the frame exactly fitted and prepared yet to bring such piece in, — in such a case, we find it impossible not to believe that Stephen and Franklin and Roger and James all understood one another from the beginning, and all worked upon a common plan or draft, drawn up before the first blow was struck.

It should not be overlooked that by the Nebraska Bill the people of a State as well as Territory were to be left " perfectly free," " subject only to the Constitution." Why mention a State? They were legislating for Territories, and not for or about States. Certainly the people of a State are and ought to be subject to the Constitution of the United States; but why is mention of this lugged into this merely territorial law? Why are the people of a Territory and the people of a State therein lumped together, and their relation to the Constitution therein treated as being precisely the same? While the opinion of the Court by Chief Justice Taney, in the Dred Scott case, and the separate opinions of all the concurring judges, expressly declare that the Constitution of the United States neither permits Congress nor a territorial legislature to exclude slavery from any United States Territory, they all omit to declare whether or not the same Constitution permits a State or the people of a State to exclude it. *Possibly* this is a mere omission; but who can be quite sure if McLean or Curtis had sought to get into the opinion a declaration of unlimited power in the people of a State to exclude slavery from their limits, — just as Chase and Mace sought to get such declaration

6

in behalf of the people of a Territory, into the Nebraska Bill, — I ask, who can be quite sure that it would not have been voted down in the one case as it had been in the other? The nearest approach to the point of declaring the power of a State over slavery is made by Judge Nelson. He approaches it more than once, using the precise idea, and almost the language too, of the Nebraska act. On one occasion his exact language is " except in cases where the power is restrained by the Constitution of the United States, the law of the State is supreme over the subject of slavery within its jurisdiction." In what cases the power of the State is so restrained by the United States Constitution is left an open question, precisely as the same question, as to the restraint on the power of the Territories, was left open in the Nebraska act. Put this and that together, and we have another nice little niche, which we may, ere long, see filled with another Supreme Court decision, declaring that the Constitution of the United States does not permit *a State* to exclude slavery from its limits. And this may especially be expected if the doctrine of " care not whether slavery be voted down or voted up " shall gain upon the public mind sufficiently to give promise that such a decision can be maintained when made.

Such a decision is all that slavery now lacks of being alike lawful in all the States. Welcome or unwelcome, such decision is probably coming, and will soon be upon us, unless the power of the present political dynasty shall be met and overthrown. We shall lie down, pleasantly dreaming that the people of Missouri are on the verge of making their State free, and we shall awake to the reality instead, that the Supreme Court has made Illinois a slave State. To meet and overthrow the power of that dynasty is the work now before all those who would prevent that consummation. That is what we have to do. How can we best do it?

There are those who denounce us openly to their own friends, and yet whisper to us softly that Senator Douglas is the aptest instrument there is with which to effect that object. They wish us to *infer* all from the fact that he now has a little quarrel with the present head of that dynasty, and that he has regularly voted with us on a single point, upon which he and we have never differed. They remind us that he is a great man and that the largest of us are very small ones. Let this be granted. But "a living dog is better than a dead lion." Judge Douglas, if not a dead lion, for this work is at least a caged and toothless one. How can he oppose the advances of slavery? He don't care anything about it. His avowed mission is impressing the "public heart" to *care nothing about it.* A leading Douglas Democratic newspaper thinks Douglas's superior talent will be needed to resist the revival of the African slave-trade. Does Douglas believe an effort to revive that trade is approaching? He has not said so. Does he really think so? But if it is, how can he resist it? For years he has laboured to prove it a sacred right of white men to take negro slaves into the new territories. Can he possibly show that it is a less sacred right to buy them where they can be bought cheapest? And unquestionably they can be bought cheaper in Africa than in Virginia. He has done all in his power to reduce the whole question of slavery to one of a mere right of property: and, as such, how can he oppose the foreign slave-trade? — how can he refuse that trade in that property shall be "perfectly free," unless he does it as a protection to home production? And as the home producers will probably not ask the protection, he will be wholly without a ground of opposition.

Senator Douglas holds, we know, that a man may rightfully be wiser to-day than he was yesterday — that he may rightfully change when he finds himself wrong. But can we, for that reason, run ahead, and infer that he will make any particular change, of which he himself has given no intimation? Can we safely base our action upon any such vague inference?

Now, as ever, I wish not to misrepresent Judge Douglas's position, question his motives, or do aught that can be personally offensive to him. Whenever, if ever, he and we can come together on principle, so that our cause may have assistance from his great ability, I hope to have interposed no adventitious obstacle. But, clearly, he is not now with us — he does not pretend to be —he does not promise ever to be.

Our cause, then, must be intrusted to, and conducted by, its own undoubted friends — those whose hands are free, whose hearts are in the work, who do care for the result. Two years ago the Republicans of the nation mustered over thirteen hundred thousand strong. We did this under the single impulse of resistance to a common danger, with every external circumstance against us. Of strange, discordant, and even hostile elements, we gathered from the four winds, and formed and fought the battle through, under the constant hot fire of a disciplined, proud, and pampered enemy.

Did we brave all then to falter now? — now,
when that same enemy is wavering, dissevered,
and belligerent? The result is not doubtful.
We shall not fail. If we stand firm, we shall not
fail. Wise counsels may accelerate or mistakes
delay it; but sooner or later the victory is sure
to come.

FROM HIS SPEECH AT CHICAGO, IN REPLY TO THE
SPEECH OF JUDGE DOUGLAS, ON THE EVENING
OF JULY 9, 1858.

July 10, 1858.

NOTE. — Twenty years after the delivery of
this speech the following account of it was given
to me by a conservative and distinguished Democrat. "I lived in Chicago at the time," he
said, "and I was a Douglas Democrat. We
loved the 'Little Giant' for his courage, and we
had a sympathy for him, for he seemed to be fighting half his own party and all the Republicans.

"I listened to Douglas's speech on the ninth
of July. He had a large audience, in full sympathy with him, and he himself was at his best.
When he concluded there were many calls for
Lincoln. He appeared, and quietly said that the
hour was late, the audience weary, and to answer
Judge Douglas one must begin earlier in the
evening. He did not know that he should be
able to answer him, but those who cared to hear
him try, would come there the next evening.

" I heard Mr. Lincoln's speech the next evening, every word of it. When I assure you that it convinced and converted a Douglas Democrat like myself, I have expressed not only my own opinion, but that of ten thousand others comprising that audience. I was satisfied then that the ' Little Giant ' had met his master."

This speech was generally considered by Republicans as second in importance only to the " Divided House " speech, the principles of which it firmly maintained. It was afterwards republished, with others, under the same cover as the Douglas and Lincoln Debate, and had a wide circulation. No apology is deemed necessary for the length of the selections from it, — it would be published entire if the portions here omitted did not appear elsewhere in this volume.

The address commenced with a good-natured refutation of the charge that an alliance to defeat Douglas existed between the friends of Lincoln and the Buchanan Democrats. Then Mr. Lincoln went straight to the Douglas war-cry of Popular Sovereignty.

" . . . Popular sovereignty! everlasting popular sovereignty! Let us for a moment inquire into this vast matter of popular sovereignty. What is popular sovereignty? We recollect that at an early period in the history of this struggle, there was another name for the same thing, — *squatter sovereignty*. It was not exactly popular sovereignty, but squatter sovereignty. What do these terms mean? What do those terms mean when used now? And vast credit is taken by our friend, the Judge, in regard to his support of it, when he declares the last years of his life have been, and all the future years of his life shall be, devoted to this matter of popular sovereignty. What is it? Why, it is the sovereignty of the people! What was squatter sovereignty? I suppose, if it had any signification at all, it was the right of the people to govern themselves, to be sovereign in their own affairs, while they were squatted down in a country not their own, — while they had squatted on a territory that did not belong to them, in the sense that a State belongs to the people who inhabit it, — when it belonged to the nation; such right to govern themselves was called 'squatter sovereignty.'

"Now, I wish you to mark, What has become of that squatter sovereignty? What has become of it? Can you get anybody to tell you now that the people of a Territory have any authority to govern themselves, in regard to this mooted question of slavery, before they form a State constitution? No such thing at all, although there is a general running fire, and although there has been a hurrah made in every speech on that side, assuming that policy had given to the people of a Territory the right to govern themselves upon this question; yet the point is dodged. To-day it has been decided — no more than a year ago it was decided by the Supreme Court of the United States, and is insisted upon to-day — that the people of a Territory have no right to exclude slavery from a Territory; that if any one man chooses to take slaves into a Territory, all the rest of the people have no right to keep them out. This being so, and this decision being made, one of the points that the Judge approved, and one in the approval of which he says he means to keep me down, — *put* me down I should not say, for I have never been up! He says he is in favour of it, and sticks to it, and expects to win his battle on that decision, which says that there is no such thing as squatter sovereignty, but that any one man may take slaves into a Territory, and all the other men in the Territory may be opposed to it, and yet by reason of the Constitution they cannot prohibit it. When that is so, how much is left of this vast matter of squatter sovereignty, I should like to know?

" When we get back, we get to the point of the right of the people to make a constitution. Kansas was settled, for example, in 1854. It was a

Territory yet, without having formed a constitution, in a very regular way, for three years. All this time negro slavery could be taken in by any few individuals, and by that decision of the Supreme Court, which the Judge approves, all the rest of the people cannot keep it out; but when they come to make a constitution they may say they will not have slavery. But it is there; they are obliged to tolerate it in some way, and all experience shows it will be so, — for they will not take the negro slaves and absolutely deprive the owners of them. All experience shows this to be so. All that space of time that runs from the beginning of the settlement of the Territory until there is a sufficiency of people to make a State constitution, — all that portion of time popular sovereignty is given up. The seal is absolutely put down upon it by the court decision, and Judge Douglas puts his own upon the top of that; yet he is appealing to the people to give him vast credit for his devotion to popular sovereignty.

"Again, when we get to the question of the right of the people to form a State constitution as they please, to form it with slavery or without slavery, — if that is anything new I confess I don't know it. Has there ever been a time when anybody said that any other than the people of

a Territory itself should form a constitution?
What is now in it that Judge Douglas should have
fought several years of his life, and pledge himself to fight all the remaining years of his life for?
Can Judge Douglas find anybody on earth that
said that anybody else should form a constitution
for a people? . . . It is enough for my purpose to ask, whenever a Republican said anything against it? They never said anything
against it, but they have constantly spoken for
it; and whosoever will undertake to examine
the platform and the speeches of responsible
men of the party, and of irresponsible men, too,
if you please, will be unable to find one word
from anybody in the Republican ranks opposed
to that popular sovereignty which Judge Douglas
thinks he has invented. I suppose that Judge
Douglas will claim in a little while that he is the
inventor of the idea that the people should govern themselves; that nobody ever thought of
such a thing until he brought it forward. We do
not remember that in that old Declaration of
Independence it is said that 'We hold these truths
to be self-evident, that all men are created equal;
that they are endowed by their Creator with
certain inalienable rights; that among these are
life, liberty, and the pursuit of happiness; that to

secure these rights, governments are instituted among men, deriving their just powers from the consent of the governed.' There is the origin of popular sovereignty. Who, then, shall come in at this day and claim that he invented it?

"The Lecompton constitution connects itself with this question, for it is in this matter of the Lecompton constitution that our friend Judge Douglas claims such vast credit. I agree that in opposing the Lecompton constitution, so far as I can perceive, he was right. I do not deny that at all; and, gentlemen, you will readily see why I could not deny it, even if I wanted to. But I do not wish to, for all the Republicans in the nation opposed it, and they would have opposed it just as much without Judge Douglas's aid as with it. They had all taken ground against it long before he did. Why, the reason that he urges against that constitution I urged against him a year before. I have the printed speech in my hand. The argument that he makes why that constitution should not be adopted, that the people were not fairly represented nor allowed to vote, I pointed out in a speech a year ago, which I hold in my hand now, that no fair chance was to be given to the people. . . .

"A little more now as to this matter of popular sovereignty and the Lecompton constitution. The Lecompton constitution, as the Judge tells us, was defeated. The defeat of it was a good thing, or it was not. He thinks the defeat of it was a good thing, and so do I; and we agree in that. Who defeated it? [A voice, "Judge Douglas."] Yes, he furnished himself; and if you suppose he controlled the other Democrats that went with him, he furnished three votes, while the Republicans furnished twenty.

"That is what he did to defeat it. In the House of Representatives he and his friends furnished some twenty votes, and the Republicans furnished ninety odd. Now, who was it that did the work? [A voice, "Douglas."] Why, yes, Douglas did it? To be sure he did!

"Let us, however, put that proposition another way. The Republicans could not have done it without Judge Douglas. Could he have done it without them? Which could have come the nearest to doing it without the other? Ground was taken against it by the Republicans long before Douglas did it. The proposition of opposition to that measure is about five to one. [A voice, "Why don't they come out on it?"] You don't know what you are talking about, my friend; I am quite willing to answer any gen-

tleman in the crowd who asks an intelligent
question.

"Now, who in all this country has ever found
any of our friends of Judge Douglas's way of
thinking, and who have acted upon this main
question, that have ever thought of uttering a
word in behalf of Judge Trumbull? I defy you
to show a printed resolution passed in a Democratic meeting. I take it upon myself to defy
any man to show a printed resolution, large or
small, of a Democratic meeting in favour of Judge
Trumbull, or any of the five to one Republicans
who beat that bill. Everything must be for the
Democrats! They did everything, and the five to
the one that really did the thing, they snub over,
and they do not seem to remember that they
have an existence upon the face of the earth.

"Gentlemen, I fear that I shall become tedious. I leave this branch of the subject to take
hold of another. I take up that part of Judge
Douglas's speech in which he respectfully attended to me.

"Judge Douglas made two points upon my
recent speech at Springfield. He says they are
to be the issues of this campaign. The first one
of these points he bases upon the language in a
speech which I delivered at Springfield, which I

believe I can quote correctly from memory. I said that ' we are now far into the fifth year since a policy was instituted for the avowed object and with the confident promise of putting an end to slavery agitation ; under the operation of that policy, that agitation has not only not ceased, but has constantly augmented. I believe it will not cease until a crisis shall have been reached and passed. "A house divided against itself cannot stand." I believe this government cannot endure permanently half slave and half free. I do not expect the Union to be dissolved,' — I am quoting from my speech, — 'I do not expect the house to fall, but I do expect it will cease to be divided. It will become all one thing or all the other. Either the opponents of slavery will arrest the further spread of it, and place it where the public mind shall rest in the belief that it is in the course of ultimate extinction, or its advocates will push it forward until it shall become alike lawful in all the States, old as well as new ; North as well as South.'

"That is the paragraph ! In this paragraph which I have quoted in your hearing, and to which I ask the attention of all, Judge Douglas thinks he discovers great political heresy. I want your attention particularly to what he has inferred from it. He says I am in favour of making all the States of this Union uniform in all their internal regulations; that in all their domestic concerns I am in favour of making them entirely uniform. He draws this inference from the language I have quoted to you. He says that I am in favour of making war by the North upon the South for the extinction of slavery; that I am also in favour of inviting (as he expresses it) the South to a war upon the North for the purpose of nationalising slavery. Now, it is singular enough, if you will carefully read that passage over, that I did not say that I was in favour of anything in it. I only said what I expected would take place. I made a prediction only, — it may have been a foolish one, perhaps. I did not even say that I desired that slavery should be put in course of ultimate extinction. I do say so now, however; so there need be no longer any difficulty about that. It may be written down in the great speech.

"Gentlemen, Judge Douglas informed you that this speech of mine was probably carefully prepared. I admit that it was. I am not master of language; I have not a fine education; I am not capable of entering into a disquisition upon dialectics, as I believe you call it; but I do not believe the language I employed bears any such construction as Judge Douglas puts upon it. But I don't care about a quibble in regard to words. I know what I meant, and I will not leave this crowd in doubt, if I can explain it to them, what I really meant in the use of that paragraph.

"I am not, in the first place, unaware that this government has endured eighty-two years, half slave and half free. I know that. I am tolerably well acquainted with the history of the country, and I know that it has endured eighty-two years, half slave and half free. I believe — and that is what I meant to allude to there — I believe it has endured, because, during all that time, until the introduction of the Nebraska Bill, the public mind did rest all the time in the belief that slavery was in course of ultimate extinction. That was what gave us the rest that we had through that period of eighty-two years ; at least, so I believe. I have always hated slavery, I think, as much as any Abolitionist, — I have been an old-line Whig, — I have always hated it, but I have always been quiet about it until this new era of the introduction of the Nebraska Bill began. I always believed that everybody was against it, and that it was in course of ultimate extinction. . . . They had reason so to believe.

"The adoption of the Constitution and its at-

tendant history led the people to believe so, and
that such was the belief of the framers of the
Constitution itself. Why did those old men,
about the time of the adoption of the Constitution, decree that slavery should not go into the
new Territory where it had not already gone?
Why declare that within twenty years the African
slave-trade, by which slaves are supplied, might
be cut off by Congress? Why were all these
acts? I might enumerate more of these acts;
but enough. What were they but a clear indication that the framers of the Constitution intended
and expected the ultimate extinction of that institution? And now when I say, — as I said in
my speech that Judge Douglas has quoted from,
— when I say that I think the opponents of
slavery will resist the further spread of it, and
place it where the public mind shall rest in the
belief that it is in the course of ultimate extinction, I only mean to say that they will place
it where the founders of this government originally placed it.

" I have said a hundred times, and I have now
no inclination to take it back, that I believe there
is no right, and ought to be no inclination in the
people of the free States, to enter into the slave
States and interfere with the question of slavery

at all. . . . And when it is said that I am in favour of interfering with slavery where it exists, I know it is unwarranted by anything I have ever intended, and, as I believe, by anything I have ever said. If by any means I have ever used language which could fairly be so construed (as, however, I believe I never have), I now correct it. . . .

" Now, in relation to his inference that I am in favour of a general consolidation of all the local institutions of the various States. . . . I have said very many times in Judge Douglas's hearing that no man believed more than I in the principle of self-government ; that it lies at the bottom of all my ideas of just government from beginning to end. . . . I deny that any man has ever gone ahead of me in his devotion to the principle, whatever he may have done in efficiency in advocating it. I think that I have said it in your hearing, that I believe each individual is naturally entitled to do as he pleases with himself and the fruit of his labour, so far as it in no wise interferes with any other man's rights ; that each community, as a State, has a right to do exactly as it pleases with all the concerns within that State that interfere with the right of no other State ; and that the general government upon principle has no right to interfere with anything other than that general class of things that does concern the whole. I have said that at all times; I have said as illustrations that I do not believe in the right of Illinois to interfere with the cranberry laws of Indiana, the oyster laws of Virginia, or the liquor laws of Maine.

"How is it, then, that Judge Douglas infers, because I hope to see slavery put where the public mind shall rest in the belief that it is in the course of ultimate extinction, that I am in favour of Illinois going over and interfering with the cranberry laws of Indiana? What can authorise him to draw any such inference? I suppose there might be one thing that at least enabled him to draw such an inference, that would not be true with me or many others; that is, because he looks upon all this matter of slavery as an exceedingly little thing, — this matter of keeping one-sixth of the population of the whole nation in a state of oppression and tyranny unequalled in the world. He looks upon it as being an exceedingly little thing, only equal to the question of the cranberry laws of Indiana; as something having no moral question in it; as something on a par with the question of whether a man shall pasture his land with cattle or plant it

with tobacco; so little and so small a thing that
he concludes, if I could desire that anything
should be done to bring about the ultimate extinction of that little thing, I must be in favour
of bringing about an amalgamation of all the
other little things in the Union. Now, it so happens — and there, I presume, is the foundation
of this mistake — that the Judge thinks thus; and
it so happens that there is a vast portion of the
American people that do not look upon that matter as being this very little thing. They look upon
it as a vast moral evil; they can prove it as such
by the writings of those who gave us the blessings
of liberty which we enjoy, and that they so looked
upon it, and not as an evil merely confining
itself to the States where it is situated; and while
we agree that by the Constitution we assented to,
in the States where it exists we have no right to
interfere with it, because it is in the Constitution,
we are both by duty and inclination to stick by
that Constitution in all its letter and spirit from
beginning to end.

"So much, then, as to my disposition, my wish,
to have all the State legislatures blotted out and
to have one consolidated government and a uniformity of domestic regulations in all the States;
by which I suppose it is meant, if we raise corn

here we must make sugar-cane grow here too, and we must make those things which grow North grow in the South. All this I suppose he understands I am in favour of doing. Now, so much for all this nonsense — for I must call it so. The Judge can have no issue with me on a question of establishing uniformity in the domestic regulations of the States.

"A little now on the other point, — the Dred Scott decision. Another of the issues, he says, that is to be made with me is upon his devotion to the Dred Scott decision and my opposition to it.

"I have expressed heretofore, and I now repeat, my opposition to the Dred Scott decision; but I should be allowed to state the nature of that opposition, and I ask your indulgence while I do so. What is fairly implied by the term Judge Douglas has used, 'resistance to the decision'? I do not resist it. If I wanted to take Dred Scott from his master I would be interfering with property, and that terrible difficulty that Judge Douglas speaks of, of interfering with property, would arise. But I am doing no such thing as that; all that I am doing is refusing to obey it as a political rule. If I were in Congress, and a vote should come up on a question whether slavery should be prohibited in a new Territory, in spite of the Dred Scott decision, I would vote that it should.

"That is what I would do. Judge Douglas said last night that before the decision he might advance his opinion, and it might be contrary to the decision when it was made ; but after it was made he would abide by it until it was reversed. Just so ! We let this property abide by the decision, but we will try to reverse that decision. We will try to put it where Judge Douglas would not object, for he says he will obey it until it is reversed. Somebody has to reverse that decision, since it is made ; and we mean to reverse it, and we mean to do it peaceably.

"What are the uses of decisions of courts? They have two uses. First, they decide upon the question before the court. They decide in this case that Dred Scott is a slave. Nobody resists that. Not only that, but they say to everybody else that persons standing just as Dred Scott stands are as he is. That is, they say that when a question comes up upon another person it will be so decided again, unless the court decides another way, unless the court overrules its decision. Well, we mean to do what we can to have the court decide the other way. That is one thing we mean to try to do.

"The sacredness that Judge Douglas throws around this decision is a degree of sacredness that has never been before thrown around any other decision. I have never heard of such a thing. Why, decisions apparently contrary to that decision, or that good lawyers thought were contrary to that decision, have been made by that very court before. It is the first of its kind; it is an astonisher in legal history; it is a new wonder of the world; it is based upon falsehood in the main as to the facts, — allegations of facts upon which it stands are not facts at all in many instances, — and no decision made on any question — the first instance of a decision made under so many unfavourable circumstances — thus placed, has ever been held by the profession as law, and it has always needed confirmation before the lawyers regarded it as settled law; but Judge Douglas will have it that all hands must take this extraordinary decision made under these extraordinary circumstances and give their vote in Congress in accordance with it, yield to it, and obey it in every possible sense. Circumstances alter cases. Do not gentlemen here remember the case of that same Supreme Court some twenty-five or thirty years ago, deciding that a national bank was constitutional? I ask if some-

body does not remember that a national bank
was declared to be constitutional? Such is the
truth, whether it be remembered or not. The
bank charter ran out, and a re-charter was granted
by Congress. That re-charter was laid before
General Jackson. It was urged upon him, when
he denied the constitutionality of the bank, that
the Supreme Court had decided that it was constitutional; and General Jackson then said that
the Supreme Court had no right to lay down a
rule to govern a co-ordinate branch of the government, the members of which had sworn to
support the Constitution, — that each member
had sworn to support the Constitution as he understood it. I will venture here to say that I
have heard Judge Douglas say that he approved
of General Jackson for that act. What has now
become of all his tirade against 'resistance to the
Supreme Court'?

"My fellow-citizens, getting back a little, — for
I pass from these points, — when Judge Douglas
makes his threat of annihilation upon the 'alliance,' he is cautious to say that that warfare of
his is to fall upon the leaders of the Republican
party. Almost every word he utters and every
distinction he makes has its significance. He
means for the Republicans who do not count

themselves as leaders to be his friends; he makes no fuss over them, it is the leaders that he is making war upon. He wants it understood that the mass of the Republican party are really his friends. It is only the leaders that are doing something, that are intolerant, and require extermination at his hands. As this is clearly and unquestionably the light in which he presents that matter, I want to ask your attention, addressing myself to Republicans here, that I may ask you some questions as to where you, as the Republican party, would be placed if you sustained Judge Douglas in his present position by a re-election? I do not claim, gentlemen, to be unselfish; I do not pretend that I would not like to go to the United States Senate, — I make no such hypocritical pretence; but I do say to you, that in this mighty issue it is nothing to you, nothing to the mass of the people of the nation, whether or not Judge Douglas or myself shall ever be heard of after this night. It may be a trifle to either of us; but in connection with this mighty question, upon which hang the destinies of the nation, perhaps, it is absolutely nothing. But where will you be placed if you reindorse Judge Douglas? Don't you know how apt he is, how exceedingly anxious he is, at all times to seize

upon anything and everything to persuade you
that something he has done you did yourselves?
Why, he tried to persuade you last night that our
Illinois Legislature instructed him to introduce
the Nebraska Bill. There was nobody in that
Legislature ever thought of it; but still he fights
furiously for the proposition; and that he did it
because there was a standing instruction to our
senators to be always introducing Nebraska bills.
He tells you he is for the Cincinnati platform;
he tells you he is for the Dred Scott decision;
he tells you — not in his speech last night, but
substantially in a former speech — that he cares
not if slavery is voted up or down; he tells you
the struggle on Lecompton is past, — it may come
up again or not, and if it does, he stands where
he stood when, in spite of him and his opposition, you built up the Republican party. If
you indorse him, you tell him you do not care
whether slavery be voted up or down, and he
will close, or try to close, your mouths with his
declaration, repeated by the day, the week, the
month, and the year. I think, in the position
in which Judge Douglas stood in opposing the
Lecompton constitution, he was right; he does
not know that it will return, but if it does we may
know where to find him; and if it does not, we

may know where to look for him, and that is on the Cincinnati platform. Now, I could ask the Republican party, after all the hard names Judge Douglas has called them by, . . . all his declarations of Black Republicanism — (by the way, we are improving, the black has got rubbed off), but with all that, if he be indorsed by Republican votes, where do you stand? Plainly, you stand ready saddled, bridled, and harnessed, and waiting to be driven over to the slavery-extension camp of the nation, — just ready to be driven over, tied together in a lot, — to be driven over, every man with a rope around his neck, that halter being held by Judge Douglas. That is the question. If Republican men have been in earnest in what they have done, I think they had better not do it; but I think the Republican party is made up of those who, as far as they can peaceably, will oppose the extension of slavery, and who will hope for its ultimate extinction. If they believe it is wrong in grasping up the new lands of the continent, and keeping them from the settlement of free white labourers, who want the land to bring up their families upon; if they are in earnest, — although they may make a mistake, they will grow restless, and the time will come when they will come back again and reorganise, if not by the same name, at least upon the same principles as their party now has. It is better, then, to save the work while it is begun. You have done the labour; maintain it, keep it. If men choose to serve you, go with them; but as you have made up your organisation upon principle, stand by it; for, as surely as God reigns over you, and has inspired your minds and given you a sense of propriety and continues to give you hope, so surely will you still cling to these ideas, and you will at last come back again after your wanderings, merely to do your work over again.

"We were often, — more than once, at least, — in the course of Judge Douglas's speech last night, reminded that this government was made for white men, — that he believed it was made for white men. Well, that is putting it into a shape in which no one wants to deny it; but the Judge then goes into his passion for drawing inferences that are not warranted. I protest, now and for ever, against that counterfeit logic which presumes that, because I do not want a negro woman for a slave, I do necessarily want her for a wife. My understanding is, that I need not have her for either; but, as God made us separate, we can leave one another alone, and do one another much good thereby. There are white men enough to marry all the white women, and enough black men to marry all the black women; and in God's name let them be so married. The Judge regales us with the terrible enormities that take place by the mixture of races; that the inferior race bears the superior down. Why, Judge, if we do not let them get together in the Territories, they won't mix there. I should say at least that that was a self-evident truth.

"Now, it happens that we meet together once every year, somewhere about the 4th of July, for some reason or other. These 4th of July gatherings, I suppose, have their uses. If you will indulge me, I will state what I suppose to be some of them.

"We are now a mighty nation : we are thirty, or about thirty, millions of people, and we own and inhabit about one-fifteenth part of the dry land of the whole earth. We run our memory back over the pages of history for about eighty-two years, and we discover that we were then a very small people in point of numbers, vastly inferior to what we are now, with a vastly less extent of country, with vastly less of everything we deem desirable among men. We look upon the change as exceedingly advantageous to us and to our posterity, and we fix upon something that happened away back, as in some way or other being connected with this rise of prosperity. We find a race of men living in that day whom we claim as our fathers and grandfathers; they were iron men; they fought for the principle that they were contending for, and we understand that by what they then did, it has followed that the degree of prosperity which we now enjoy has come to us. We hold this annual celebration to remind ourselves of all the good done in this process of time, — of how it was done, and who did it, and how we are historically connected with it; and we go from these meetings in better humour with ourselves, — we feel more attached the one to the other, and more firmly bound to the country we inhabit. In every way we are better men, in the age and race and country in which we live, for these celebrations. But after we have done all this, we have not yet reached the whole. There is something else connected with it. We have, besides these men — descended by blood from our ancestors — among us, perhaps half our people who are not descendants at all of these men; they are men who have come from Europe, — German, Irish, French, and Scandinavian, — men that have come from Europe themselves, or whose ancestors have come hither and settled here, finding themselves our equal in all things. If they look back through this history, to trace their connection with those days by blood, they find they have none : they cannot carry themselves back into that glorious epoch and make themselves feel that they are part of us ; but when they look through that old Declaration of Independence, they find that those old men say that 'we hold these truths to be self-evident, that all men are created equal,' and then they feel that that moral sentiment taught in that day evidences their relation to those men, that it is the father of all moral principle in them, and that they have a right to claim it as though they were blood of the blood, and flesh of the flesh, of the men who wrote that Declaration ; and so they are. That is the electric cord in that Declaration that links the hearts of patriotic and liberty-loving men together ; that will link those patriotic hearts as long as the love of freedom exists in the minds of men throughout the world.

"Now, sirs, for the purpose of squaring things with this idea of ' don't care if slavery is voted up or voted down ;' for sustaining the Dred Scott decision ; for holding that the Declaration of Independence did not mean anything at all, — we have Judge Douglas giving his exposition of what the Declaration of Independence means, and we have him saying that the people of America are equal to the people of England. According to his construction, you Germans are not connected with it. Now, I ask you in all soberness, if all these things, if indulged in, if ratified, if confirmed and indorsed, if taught to our children and repeated to them, do not tend to rub out the sentiment of liberty in the country, and to transform this government into a government of some other form? Those arguments that are made, that the inferior race are to be treated with as much allowance as they are capable of enjoying; that as much is to be done for them as their condition will allow,— what are these arguments? They are the arguments that kings have made for enslaving the people in all ages of the world. You will find that all the arguments in favour of kingcraft were of this class; they always bestrode the necks of the people, — not that they wanted to do it, but because the people were better off for being ridden. That is their argument; and this argument of the Judge is the same old serpent, that says, 'You work, and I eat; you toil, and I will enjoy the fruits of it.' Turn in whatever way you will,— whether it come from the

8

mouth of a king, an excuse for enslaving the people of his country, or from the mouth of men of one
race as a reason for enslaving the men of another
race, — it is all the same old serpent; and I hold,
if that course of argumentation that is made for
the purpose of convincing the public mind that
we should not care about this, should be granted,
it does not stop with the negro. I should like to
know — taking this old Declaration of Independence, which declares that all men are equal,
upon principle, and making exceptions to it —
where will it stop? If one man says it does not
mean a negro, why not another say it does not
mean some other man? If that Declaration is
not the truth, let us get the statute-book in which
we find it, and tear it out! Who is so bold as to
do it? If it is not true, let us tear it out. [Cries
of " No! No!"] Let us stick to it, then; let us
stand firmly by it, then.

"It may be argued that there are certain conditions that make necessities and impose them
upon us, and to the extent that a necessity is
imposed upon a man, he must submit to it. I
think that was the condition in which we found
ourselves when we established this government.
We had slaves among us; we could not get our
Constitution unless we permitted them to remain

in slavery; we could not secure the good we did secure, if we grasped for more; but, having by necessity submitted to that much, it does not destroy the principle that is the charter of our liberties. Let that charter stand as our standard.

"My friend has said to me that I am a poor hand to quote Scripture. I will try it again, however. It is said in one of the admonitions of our Lord, 'Be ye [therefore] perfect even as your Father which is in heaven is perfect.' The Saviour, I suppose, did not expect that any human creature could be perfect as the Father in heaven; but He said: 'As your Father in heaven is perfect, be ye also perfect.' He set that up as a standard, and he who did most toward reaching that standard attained the highest degree of moral perfection. So I say in relation to the principle that all men are created equal, let it be as nearly reached as we can. If we cannot give freedom to every creature, let us do nothing that will impose slavery upon any other creature. Let us, then, turn this government back into the channel in which the framers of the Constitution originally placed it. Let us stand firmly by each other. If we do not do so, we are tending in the contrary direction, that our friend Judge Douglas proposes, — not intentionally, — working in the traces that tend to make this one universal slave nation. He is one that runs in that direction, and as such I resist him.

"My friends, I have detained you about as long as I desired to do, and I have only to say, let us discard all this quibbling about this man and the other man, this race and that race and the other race being inferior, and therefore they must be placed in an inferior position. Let us discard all these things, and unite as one people throughout this land, until we shall once more stand up declaring that all men are created equal.

"My friends, I could not, without launching off upon some new topic, which would detain you too long, continue to-night. I thank you for this most extensive audience that you have furnished me to-night. I leave you, hoping that the lamp of liberty will burn in your bosoms until there shall no longer be a doubt that all men are created free and equal."

From his Speech at Springfield, Illinois.

July 17, 1858.

" . . . There is still another disadvantage under which we labour, and to which I will ask your attention. It arises out of the relative positions of the two persons who stand before the State as candidates for the Senate. Senator Douglas is of world-wide renown. All the anxious politicians of his party, or who have been of his party for years past, have been looking upon him as certainly, at no distant day, to be the President of the United States. They have seen, in his round, jolly, fruitful face, post-offices, land-offices, marshalships, and cabinet appointments, chargé-ships and foreign missions, bursting and sprouting out in wonderful exuberance, ready to be laid hold of by their greedy hands. And as they have been gazing upon this attractive picture so long, they cannot, in the little distraction that has taken place in the party, bring themselves to give up the charming hope. But with greedier anxiety they rush about him, sustain him, and give him marches, triumphal entries, and receptions, be-yond what, even in the days of his highest pros-perity, they could have brought about in his favour. On the contrary, nobody has ever expected me to be President. In my poor, lean, lank face, nobody has ever seen that any cabbages were sprouting out. These are disadvantages, all taken together, that the Republicans labour under. We have to fight this battle upon principle, and upon principle alone. I am in a certain sense made the standard-bearer in behalf of the Republicans. I was made so merely because there had to be some one so placed, — I being in no wise preferable to any other one of the twenty-five, perhaps a hundred, we have in the Republican ranks. Then I say, I wish it to be distinctly understood and borne in mind, that we have to fight this battle without many — perhaps without any — of the external aids which are brought to bear against us. So I hope those with whom I am surrounded have principle enough to nerve themselves for the task, and leave nothing undone that can fairly be done to bring about the right result.

"After Senator Douglas left Washington . . . he tarried . . . in the city of New York; and it was heralded that, like another Napoleon, he was lying by and framing the plan of his campaign; . . . his plan for the purpose of going to Illinois, to pounce upon and annihilate the treasonable and disunion speech which Lincoln had made

here on the sixteenth of June. . . . I think
I have been able to see what are the material
points of that plan. . . . What I shall point out,
though not showing the whole plan, are nevertheless the main points, as I suppose.

" They are not very numerous. The first is
popular sovereignty. The second and third are
attacks upon my speech of the sixteenth of June.
. . . Auxiliary to these main points, to be sure,
are their thunderings of cannon, their marching
and music, their fizzlegigs and fireworks; but I
will not waste time with them. . . .

" As appears by two speeches I have heard
him deliver since his arrival in Illinois, he gave
special attention to the speech of mine delivered
on the sixteenth of June. He says that he carefully read that speech. He told us that at Chicago
a week ago last night, and he repeated it at Bloomington last night. . . .

" Having made that speech with the most
kindly feelings toward Judge Douglas, as mani-
fested therein, I was gratified when I found that
he had carefully examined it, and had detected
no error of fact, nor any inference against him,
nor any misrepresentations, of which he thought
fit to complain. . . . He seizes upon the doctrines he supposes to be included in that speech,

and declares that upon them will turn the issues of the campaign. He then quotes, or attempts to quote, from my speech. I will not say that he wilfully misquotes, but he does fail to quote accurately. His attempt at quoting is from a passage which I believe I can quote accurately from memory. I shall make the quotation now, with some comments upon it, as I have already said, in order that the Judge shall be left entirely without excuse for misrepresenting me. I do so now, as I hope, for the last time. I do this in great caution, in order that if he repeats his misrepresentation, it shall be plain to all that he does so wilfully. If, after all, he still persists, I shall be compelled to reconstruct the course I have marked out for myself, and draw upon such humble resources as I have for a new course, better suited to the real exigencies of the case. I set out in this campaign with the intention of conducting it strictly as a gentleman, in substance at least, if not in the outside polish. The latter I shall never be, but that which constitutes the inside of a gentleman I hope I understand, and am not less inclined to practise than others. It was my purpose and expectation that this canvass would be conducted upon principle, and with fairness on both sides, and it shall not be my fault if this purpose and expectation shall be given up.

"He charges, in substance, that I invite a war of sections; that I propose all local institutions of the different States shall become consolidated and uniform. What is there in the language of that speech which expresses such purpose or bears such construction? I have again and again said that I would not enter into any one of the States to disturb the institution of slavery. Judge Douglas said at Bloomington that I used language most able and ingenious for concealing what I really meant; and that while I had protested against entering into the slave States, I nevertheless did mean to go on the banks of the Ohio and throw missiles into Kentucky, to disturb them in their domestic institutions.

"I said in that speech, and I meant no more, that the institution of slavery ought to be placed in the very attitude where the framers of this government placed it. . . . In the sentence referred to, I simply expressed an expectation. Cannot the Judge perceive a distinction between a purpose and an expectation? I have often expressed an expectation to die, but I have never expressed a wish to die. . . . I said at Chicago, and I now repeat, that I do wish to see the spread of slavery arrested, and to see it placed where the public mind shall rest in the belief that it is in the course of ultimate extinction . . . then . . . we shall have peace on the slavery question.

" . . . I have said that I do not understand the Declaration to mean that all men were created equal in all respects. The negroes are not our equals in colour; but I suppose it does mean to declare that all men are equal in some respects; they are equal in their right to 'life, liberty, and the pursuit of happiness.' Certainly the negro is not our equal in colour, perhaps not in many other respects. Still, in the right to put into his mouth the bread that his own hands have earned, he is the equal of every other man, white or black. In pointing out that more has been given you, you cannot be justified in taking away the little which has been given him. All I ask for the negro is, that if you do not like him, let him alone. If God gave him but little, that little let him enjoy.

" . . . One more point on this Springfield speech, which Judge Douglas says he has read so carefully. I expressed my belief in the existence of a conspiracy to perpetuate and national-ise slavery. I did not profess to know it, nor do I now. I showed the part Judge Douglas had played in the string of facts, constituting to my mind the proof of that conspiracy. I showed the parts played by others.

"I charged that the people had been deceived into carrying the last presidential election, by the impression that the people of the Territories might exclude slavery if they chose, when it was known in advance by the conspirators that the court was to decide that neither Congress nor the people could so exclude slavery. These charges are more distinctly made than anything else in the speech.

"Judge Douglas has carefully read and re-read that speech. He has not, so far as I know, contradicted those charges. In the two speeches which I heard he certainly did not. On his own tacit admission I renew that charge. I charge him with having been a party to that conspiracy and to that deception, for the sole purpose of nationalizing slavery."

THE LINCOLN AND DOUGLAS DEBATE.

THE FIRST MEETING AT OTTAWA, ILLINOIS.

August 21, 1858.

[In his opening speech, Judge Douglas formulated the direct charge of a conspiracy created in 1854, between Mr. Lincoln and Judge Lyman Trumbull and their followers, to dissolve the old national Whig and Democratic parties, and to form out of the materials a new sectional, Abolition party, which should reward both the leaders by an election to the Senate of the United States. He said that their platform was adopted in a convention held at Springfield in October, 1854, some resolutions of which he read. He concluded as follows :]

" . . . I believe that this new doctrine preached by Mr. Lincoln and his party will dissolve the Union if it succeeds. They are trying to array all the Northern States in one body against the South ; to excite a sectional war between the free States and the slave States, in order that the one or the other may be driven to the wall."

Mr. Lincoln began his reply by saying : —

" When a man hears himself somewhat misrepresented, it provokes him — at least, I find it so with myself ; but when misrepresentation becomes very gross and palpable, it is more apt to amuse him. . . . [After stating the charge of an arrangement between himself and Judge Trumbull.]

"Now, all I have to say upon that subject is, that I think no man — not even Judge Douglas — can prove it, because it is not true. I have no doubt he is 'conscientious' in saying it. As to those resolutions that he took such a length of time to read, as being the platform of the Republican party in 1854, I say I never had anything to do with them, and I think Trumbull never had. . . .

"Now, about this story that Judge Douglas tells of Trumbull bargaining to sell out the old Democratic party, and Lincoln agreeing to sell out the old Whig party, I have the means of knowing about that; Judge Douglas cannot have; and I know there is no substance to it whatever. . . .

"A man cannot prove a negative, but he has a right to claim that when a man makes an affirmative charge, he must offer some proof to show the truth of what he says. I certainly cannot introduce testimony to show the negative about things, but I have a right to claim that if a man says he knows a thing, then he must show how he knows it. I always have a right to claim this; and it is not satisfactory to me that he may be 'conscientious' on the subject.

" . . . In regard to that general abolition tilt that Judge Douglas makes, when he says that I was engaged at that time in Abolitionizing the old Whig party, I hope you will permit me to read a part of a printed speech which I then made at Peoria, which will show altogether a different view of the position I took in that contest of 1854. . . .

[After reading from the Peoria speech his argument against the repeal of the Missouri Compromise, the wrong of letting slavery into Kansas and Nebraska, his hatred of the wrong and injustice of slavery, and his full recognition of the rights of the South under the Constitution, "not grudgingly, but fully and fairly," including "legislation for the reclamation of their fugitive slaves," — he continued :]

" . . . I have read to you the true complexion of all I have ever said in regard to the institution of slavery and the black race. This is the whole of it, and anything that argues me into his idea of perfect social and political equality with the negro is but a specious and fantastic arrangement of words, by which a man can prove a horse-chestnut to be a chestnut horse. I will say here, while upon this subject, that I have no purpose, either directly or indirectly, to interfere with the institution of slavery in the States where it exists. I believe I have no lawful right to do so, and I have no inclination to do so. I have no purpose to introduce political and social equality between the white and the black races. There is a physical difference between the two, which, in my judgment, will probably forever forbid their living together upon the footing of perfect equality; and inasmuch as it becomes a necessity that there must be a difference, I, as well as Judge Douglas, am in favour of the race to which I belong having the superior position. I have never said anything to the contrary; but I hold, that, notwithstanding all this, there is no reason in the world why the negro is not entitled to all the natural rights enumerated in the Declaration of Independence, — the right to life, liberty, and the pursuit of happiness. I hold that he is as much entitled to these as the white man. I agree with Judge Douglas, he is not my equal in many respects, certainly not in colour, perhaps not in moral or intellectual endowment. But in the right to eat the bread, without the leave of anybody, which his own hand earns, he is my equal, and the equal of Judge Douglas, and the equal of any living man.

" . . . I will dwell a little longer upon one or two of these minor topics upon which the Judge has spoken. He has read from my speech at Springfield, in which I say that 'a house divided against itself cannot stand.' Does the Judge say it can stand? I don't know whether he does or not. The Judge does not seem to be attending to me just now, but I would like to know if it is his opinion that a house divided against itself can stand? If he does, then there is a question of veracity, not between him and me, but between the Judge and an authority of a somewhat higher character.

"Now, my friends, I ask your attention to this matter for the purpose of saying something seriously. I know that the Judge may readily enough agree with me that the maxim which was put forth by the Saviour is true, but he may allege that I misapply it; and the Judge has a right to urge that in my application I do misapply it, and then I have a right to show that I do not misapply it. When he undertakes to say that because I think this nation, so far as the question of slavery is concerned, will all become one thing or all the other, I am in favour of bringing about a dead uniformity in the various States, in all their institutions, he argues erroneously. The great variety of local institutions in the States, springing from differences in the soil, differences in the face of the country, and in the climate are bonds of union. They do not make 'a house divided against itself,' but they make a house united. If they produce in one section of the country what is called for by the wants of another section, and this other section can supply the wants of the first, they are not matters of discord, but bonds of union, true bonds of union. But can this question of slavery be considered as among these varieties in the institutions of the country? I leave it for you to say, whether in the history of our government, this institution of slavery has not always failed to be a bond of union, and, on the contrary, been an apple of discord and an element of division in the house. I ask you to consider whether so long as the moral constitution of men's minds shall continue to be the same, after this generation and assemblage shall sink into the grave, and another race shall arise with the same moral and intellectual development we have — whether, if that institution is standing in the same irritating position in which it now is, it will not continue an element of division?

"If so, then I have a right to say that, in regard to this question, the Union is a house divided against itself; and when the Judge reminds me that I have often said to him that the institution of slavery has existed for eighty years in some States, and yet it does not exist in some others, I agree to the fact, and I account for it by looking at the position in which our fathers originally placed it, — restricting it from the new Territories where it had not gone, and legislating to cut off its source by the abrogation of the slave-trade, thus putting the seal of legislation against its spread. The public mind did rest in the belief that it was in the course of ultimate extinction. But lately, I think, — and in this I charge nothing on the Judge's motives, — lately, I think that he and those acting with him have placed that institution on a new basis, which looks to the perpetuity and nationalization of slavery. And while it is placed on this new basis, I say, and I have said, that I believe we shall not have peace upon the question, until the opponents of slavery arrest the further spread of it, and place it where the public mind shall rest in the belief that it is in the course of ultimate extinction ; or, on the other hand, that its advocates will push it forward until it shall become alike lawful in all the States, old as well as new, North as well as South. Now, I believe if we could arrest the spread, and place it where Washington and

Jefferson and Madison placed it, it would be in the course of ultimate extinction, and the public mind would, as for eighty years past, believe that it was in the course of ultimate extinction. The crisis would be past, and the institution might be let alone for a hundred years — if it should live so long — in the States where it exists, yet it would be going out of existence in the way best for both the black and the white races. [A voice, "Then do you repudiate popular sovereignty?"] Well, then, let us talk about popular sovereignty. What is popular sovereignty? Is it the right of the people to have slavery or not to have it, as they see fit, in the Territories? I will state — and I have an able man to watch me — my understanding is that popular sovereignty, as now applied to the question of slavery, does allow the people of a Territory to have slavery if they want to, but does not allow them not to have it if they do not want it. I do not mean that if this vast concourse of people were in a Territory of the United States, any one of them would be obliged to have a slave if he did not want one; but I do say that, as I understand the Dred Scott decision, if any one man wants slaves, all the rest have no way of keeping that one man from holding them.

"When I made my speech at Springfield, of which the Judge complains, and from which he quotes, I really was not thinking of the things which he ascribes to me at all. I had no thought in the world that I was doing anything to bring about a war between the free and slave States. I had no thought in the world that I was doing anything to bring about a political and social equality of the black and white races. It never occurred to me that I was doing anything or favouring anything to reduce to a dead uniformity all the local institutions of the various States. But I must say, in all fairness to him, if he thinks I am doing something which leads to these bad results, it is none the better that I did not mean it. It is just as fatal to the country, if I have any influence in producing it, whether I intend it or not. But can it be true that placing this institution upon the original basis — the basis upon which our fathers placed it — can have any tendency to set the Northern and the Southern States at war with one another, or that it can have any tendency to make the people of Vermont raise sugar-cane, because they raise it in Louisiana, or that it can compel the people of Illinois to cut pine logs on the Grand Prairie, where they will not grow, because they cut pine logs in Maine, where they do grow? The Judge says this is a new principle started in regard to this question. Does the Judge claim that he is working on the plan of the founders of the government? I think he says in some of his speeches — indeed, I have one here now — that he saw evidence of a policy to allow slavery to be south of a certain line, while north of it it should be excluded, and he saw an indisposition on the part of the country to stand upon that policy, and, therefore, he set about studying the subject upon original principles, and upon original principles he got up the Nebraska Bill! I am fighting it upon these 'original principles' — fighting it in the Jeffersonian, Washingtonian, Madisonian fashion.

[Mr. Lincoln then adverted to his claim made in the "Divided House" speech, that the Nebraska Bill was prepared in anticipation of the decision in the Dred Scott case, which decision denied the right of the people of a Territory to exclude slavery, which right was affirmed in the Nebraska Bill, and continued:]

" . . . I want to ask your attention to a portion of the Nebraska Bill which Judge Douglas has quoted: 'It being the true intent and meaning of this act, not to legislate slavery into any Territory or State, nor to exclude it therefrom, but to leave the people thereof perfectly free to form and regulate their domestic institutions in their own way, subject only to the Constitution of the United States.' Thereupon Judge Douglas and others began to argue in favour of ' popular sovereignty,' — the right of the people to have slaves if they wanted them, and to exclude slavery if they did not want them. ' But,' said, in substance, a senator from Ohio (Mr. Chase, I believe), ' we more than suspect that you do not mean to allow the people to exclude slavery if they wish to ; and if you do mean it, accept an amendment which I propose, expressly authorising the people to exclude slavery.' I believe I have the amendment here before me, which was offered, and under which the people of the Territory, through their proper representatives, might, if they saw fit, prohibit the existence of slavery therein. And now I state it as a fact, to be taken back if there is any mistake about it, that Judge Douglas and those acting with him voted that amendment down. I now think that those who voted it down had a real reason for doing so. They know what that reason was. It looks to us, since we have seen the Dred Scott decision pronounced, holding that ' under the Constitution ' the people cannot exclude slavery — I say it looks to outsiders, poor, simple, ' amiable, intelligent gentlemen,' as though the niche was left as a place to put that Dred Scott decision in, a niche that would have been spoiled by adopting the amendment. And now I say again, if this was not the reason, it will avail the Judge much more to calmly and good-humouredly point out to these people what that other reason was for voting the amendment down, than swelling himself up to vociferate that he may be provoked to call somebody a liar.

" Again, there is in that same quotation from the Nebraska Bill this clause : ' it being the true intent and meaning of this bill not to legislate slavery into any Territory or State.' I have always been puzzled to know what business the word ' State ' had in that connection. Judge Douglas knows — he put it there. He knows what he put it there for. We outsiders cannot say what he put it there for. The law they were passing was not about States, and was not making provision for States. What was it placed there for? After seeing the Dred Scott decision, which holds that the people cannot exclude slavery from a Territory, if another Dred Scott decision shall come, holding that they cannot exclude it from a

State, we shall discover that when the word was originally put there, it was in view of something that was to come in due time; we shall see that it was the other half of something. I now say again, if there was any different reason for putting it there, Judge Douglas, in a good-humoured way, without calling anybody a liar, can tell what the reason was.

.   .   .   .

" Now, my friends, . . . I ask the attention of the people here assembled, and elsewhere, to the course that Judge Douglas is pursuing every day as bearing upon this question of making slavery national. Not going back to the records, but taking the speeches he makes, the speeches he made yesterday and the day before, and makes constantly, all over the country, I ask your attention to them. In the first place, what is necessary to make the institution national? Not war: there is no danger that the people of Kentucky will shoulder their muskets and . . . march into Illinois to force the blacks upon us. There is no danger of our going over there, and making war upon them. Then what is necessary for the nationalization of slavery? It is simply the next Dred Scott decision. It is merely for the Supreme Court to decide that no State under the Constitution can exclude it, just as they have already decided that under the Constitution neither Congress nor the territorial legislature can do it. When that is decided and acquiesced in, the whole thing is done. This being true and this being the way, as I think, that slavery is to be made national, let us consider what Judge Douglas is doing every day to that end. In the first place, let us see what influence he is exerting on public sentiment. In this and like communities, public sentiment is everything. With public sentiment nothing can fail; without it nothing can succeed. Consequently he who moulds public sentiment goes deeper than he who enacts statutes or pronounces decisions. He makes statutes and decisions possible or impossible to be executed. This must be borne in mind, as also the additional fact that Judge Douglas is a man of vast influence, so great that it is enough for many men to profess to believe anything when they once find out that Judge Douglas professes to believe it. Consider also the attitude he occupies at the head of a large party, — a party which he claims has a majority of all the voters in the country.

"This man sticks to a decision which forbids the people of a Territory to exclude slavery, and he does so not because he says it is right in itself, — he does not give any opinion on that, — but because it has been decided by the Court, and, being decided by the Court, he is, and you are, bound to take it in your political action as law, — not that he judges at all of its merits, but because a decision of the Court is to him a 'Thus saith the Lord.' He places it on that ground alone, and you will bear in mind that thus committing himself unreservedly to this decision, commits himself just as firmly to the next one as to this. He did not commit himself on account of the merit or demerit of the decision, but it is a 'Thus saith the Lord.' The next decision as much as this will be a 'Thus saith the Lord.' There is nothing that can divert or turn him away from this decision. It is nothing that I point out to him that his great prototype, General Jackson, did not believe in the binding force of decisions. It is nothing to him that Jefferson did not so believe. I have said that I have often heard him approve of Jackson's course in disregarding the decision of the Supreme Court pronouncing a national bank constitutional. He says I did not hear him say so. He denies the accuracy of my recollection. I say he ought to know better than I, but I will make no question about this thing, though it still seems to me that I heard him say it twenty times. I will tell him, though, that he now claims to stand on the Cincinnati platform, which affirms that Congress cannot charter a national bank in the teeth of that old standing decision that Congress can charter a bank. And I remind him of another piece of Illinois history on the question of respect for judicial decisions, . . . belonging to a time when a large party to which Judge Douglas belonged, were displeased with a decision of the Supreme Court of Illinois, . . . and I know that Judge Douglas will not deny that he was then in favour of over-slaughing that decision, by the mode of adding five new Judges, so as to vote down the four old ones. Not only so, but it ended in the Judge's sitting down on the very bench as one of the five new judges to break down the four old ones. It was in this way precisely that he got his title of Judge. Now, when the Judge tells me that men appointed conditionally to sit as members of a Court will have to be catechised beforehand upon some subject, I say, ' You know, Judge ; you have tried it ! ' When he says a Court of this kind will lose the confidence of all men, will be prostituted and disgraced by such a proceeding, I say, ' You know best, Judge ; you have been through the mill.'

"But I cannot shake Judge Douglas's teeth loose from the Dred Scott decision. Like some obstinate animal (I mean no disrespect) that will hang on when he has once got his teeth fixed — you may cut off a leg, or you may tear away an arm, still he will not relax his hold. And so I may point out to the Judge, and say that he is bespattered all over, from the beginning of his political life to the present time, with attacks upon judicial decisions, — I may cut off limb after limb of his public record, and strive to wrench from him a single dictum of the Court, yet I cannot divert him from it. He hangs to the last to the Dred Scott decision. . . . Henry Clay, my beau ideal of a statesman, . . . once said of a class of men who would repress all tendencies to liberty and ultimate emancipation, that they must, if they would do this, go back to the era of our independence, and muzzle the cannon that thunders its annual joyous return; that they must blow out the moral lights around us; they must penetrate the human soul, and eradicate there the love of liberty; and then, and not till then, could they perpetuate slavery in this country! To my thinking, Judge Douglas is, by his example and vast influence, doing that very thing in this community when he says that the negro has nothing in the Declaration of Independence. Henry Clay plainly understood the contrary. Judge Douglas is going back to the era of our Revolution, and, to the extent of his ability, muzzling the cannon which thunders its annual joyous return. When he invites any people, willing to have slavery, to establish it, he is blowing out the moral lights around us. When he says he ' cares not whether slavery is voted down or voted up,'— that it is a sacred right of self-government, — he is, in my judgment, penetrating the human soul and eradicating the light of reason and the love of liberty in this American people. And now I will only say, that when, by all these means and appliances, Judge Douglas shall succeed in bringing public sentiment to an exact accordance with his own views; when these vast assemblages shall echo back all these sentiments; when they shall come to repeat his views and avow his principles, and to say all that he says on these mighty questions,— then it needs only the formality of a second Dred Scott decision, which he indorses in advance, to make slavery alike lawful in all the States, old as well as new, North as well as South."

From the Debate at Freeport, Illinois.

August 27, 1858.

[Note. — Mr. Lincoln had often said that the answer of Judge Douglas to his question whether under the Dred Scott decision the people of a Territory could exclude slavery from it before a State constitution was formed, would ruin his prospects as a candidate for the presidency. If he answered that they could, it would ruin him at the South ; if he said they could not, it would destroy his prospects in the free States. It was the opinion of Elihu B. Washburne, in whose district the Freeport meeting was held, that his answers to this and other questions of Mr. Lincoln "sounded the political death-knell of Judge Douglas." His answer was that in his opinion "the people of a Territory can, by lawful means, exclude slavery from their limits prior to the formation of a State constitution." This answer, which denied the effect of the Dred Scott decision, as claimed by the Democracy of the South, wrought the ruin predicted for it. This fact gives a greater importance to the meeting at Freeport than to all the meetings subsequently held.

In his opening speech at Freeport, Mr. Lincoln made direct answers to the seven questions which Judge Douglas had put to him at Ottawa, with such explanations as served to make his answers more full and explicit. His four questions to

Judge Douglas involved the decision in the Dred Scott case, and required him to answer whether he would vote to admit Kansas without waiting for the number of inhabitants required by the English bill; whether the people of a Territory could in any lawful way exclude slavery from its limits; whether if the Supreme Court should decide that a State could not exclude slavery, he would acquiesce in and follow such decision as a rule of political action; and whether he was in favour of acquiring additional territory, in disregard of how such acquisition would affect the slavery question. Then, after correcting some erroneous statements of fact made by his adversary, he said : —]

" . . . I have been in the habit of charging, as a matter of belief on my part, that, in the introduction of the Nebraska Bill into Congress, there was a conspiracy to make slavery perpetual and national. I have arranged, from time to time, the evidence which establishes and proves the truth of this charge. I recurred to this charge at Ottawa. I shall not now have time to dwell upon it at any great length; but inasmuch as Judge Douglas, in his reply of half an hour, made some points upon me in relation to it, I propose noticing a few of them.

" The Judge insists that in the first speech I made, in which I very distinctly made that charge, he thought for a good while that I was in fun, that I was playful, that I was not sincere about it ; and that he only grew angry and somewhat excited when he found that I insisted upon it as a matter of earnestness. He says he characterised it as a falsehood, as far as I implicated his moral character in that transaction. Well, I did not know, till he presented that view, that I had implicated his moral character. He is very much in the habit when he argues me up into a position I never thought of occupying, of very cosily saying he has no doubt Lincoln is ' conscientious ' in that matter. I can conceive it possible for men to conspire to do a good thing, and I really find nothing in Judge Douglas's course of arguments that is contrary to or inconsistent with his belief of a conspiracy to nationalize and spread slavery as being a good and blessed thing, and so I hope he will understand that I do not question but that in all this matter he is entirely ' conscientious.'

" But to draw your attention to one of the points I made in this case, beginning at the beginning : when the Nebraska Bill was introduced, or a short time afterward, by an amendment, I believe, it was provided that it must be considered ' the true intent and meaning of this act not to legislate slavery into any State or Terri-

tory, or to exclude it therefrom, but to leave the
people thereof perfectly free to form and regulate
their domestic institutions in their own way, subject only to the Constitution of the United States.'
I have called his attention to the fact that when
he and some others began arguing that they were
giving an increased degree of liberty to the people
in the Territories over and above what they formerly had on the question of slavery, a question
was raised whether the law was enacted to give
such unconditional liberty to the people ; and to
test the sincerity of this mode of argument, Mr.
Chase, of Ohio, introduced an amendment in
which he made the law — if the amendment
were adopted — expressly declare that the people
of the Territory should have the power to exclude
slavery if they saw fit. I have asked attention
also to the fact that Judge Douglas and those who
acted with him voted that amendment down, notwithstanding it expressed exactly the thing they
said was the true intent and meaning of the law.
I have called attention to the fact that in subsequent times a decision of the Supreme Court
has been made, in which it has been declared
that a Territorial Legislature has no constitutional
right to exclude slavery. And I have argued and
said that for men who did intend that the people

10

of the Territory should have the right to exclude
slavery absolutely and unconditionally, the voting
down of Chase's amendment is wholly inexpli-
cable. It is a puzzle — a riddle. But I have
said that with men who did look forward to such
a decision, or who had it in contemplation that
such a decision of the Supreme Court would or
might be made, the voting down of that amendment would be perfectly rational and intelligible.
It would keep Congress from coming in collision
with the decision when it was made. Anybody
can conceive that if there was an intention or
expectation that such a decision was to follow,
it would not be a very desirable party attitude
to get into for the Supreme Court — all, or nearly
all its members belonging to the same party — to
decide one way, when the party in Congress had
decided the other way. Hence it would be very
rational for men expecting such a decision to
keep the niche in that law clear for it. After
pointing this out, I tell Judge Douglas that it
looks to me as though here was the reason why
Chase's amendment was voted down. I tell him
that as he did it, and knows why he did it, if it
was done for a reason different from this, he
knows what that reason was, and can tell us what
it was. I tell him, also, it will be vastly more

satisfactory to the country for him to give some other plausible, intelligible reason why it was voted down, than to stand upon his dignity and call people liars. . . ."

In Mr. Lincoln's Rejoinder to Judge Douglas at Freeport, among other things, he said : —

". . . At the introduction of the Nebraska policy, we believed there was a new era being introduced in the history of the Republic, which tended to the spread and perpetuation of slavery. But in our opposition to that measure we did not agree with one another in everything. The people in the north end of the State were for stronger measures of opposition than we of the southern and central portions of the State, but we were all opposed to the Nebraska doctrine. We had that one feeling and one sentiment in common. You at the north end met in your conventions, and passed your resolutions. We in the middle of the State and further south did not hold such conventions and pass the same resolutions, although we had in general a common view and a common sentiment. So that these meetings which the Judge has alluded to, and the resolutions he has read from, were local, and did not spread over the whole State. We at last met together in 1856, from all parts of the State, and we agreed upon a common platform. You who held more extreme notions, either yielded those notions, or if not wholly yielding them, agreed to yield them practically, for the sake of embodying the opposition to the measures which the opposite party were pushing forward at that time. We met you then, and if there was anything yielded, it was for practical purposes. We agreed then upon a platform for the party throughout the entire State of Illinois, and now we are all bound as a party to that platform. And I say here to you, if any one expects of me in the case of my election, that I will do anything not signified by our Republican platform and my answers here to-day, I tell you very frankly, that person will be deceived. I do not ask for the vote of any one who supposes that I have secret purposes or pledges that I dare not speak out. . . . If I should never be elected to any office, I trust I may go down with no stain of falsehood upon my reputation, notwithstanding the hard opinions Judge Douglas chooses to entertain of me. . . . "

September 15, 1858.

" . . . I hold myself under constitutional obligations to allow the people in all the States, without interference, direct or indirect, to do exactly as they please, and I deny that I have any inclination to interfere with them, even if there were no such constitutional obligation. I can only say again that I am placed improperly — altogether improperly, in spite of all that I can say — when it is insisted that I entertain any other view or purpose in regard to that matter.

"While I am upon this subject, I will make some answers briefly to certain propositions that Judge Douglas has put. He says, ' Why can't this Union endure permanently half slave and half free ? ' I have said that I supposed it could not, and I will try, before this new audience, to give briefly some of the reasons for entertaining that opinion. Another form of his question is, 'Why can't we let it stand as our fathers placed it ? ' That is the exact difficulty between us. I say that Judge Douglas and his friends have changed it from the position in which our fathers originally placed it. I say in the way our fathers originally left the slavery question, the institution was in the course of ultimate extinction. I say when this government was first established, it was the policy of its founders to prohibit the spread of slavery into the new Territories of the United States where it had not existed. But Judge Douglas and his friends have broken up that policy, and placed it upon a new basis, by which it is to become national and perpetual. All I have asked or desired anywhere is that it should be placed back again upon the basis that the fathers of our government originally placed it upon. I have no doubt that it would become extinct for all time to come, if we had but readopted the policy of the fathers by restricting it to the limits it has already covered — restricting it from the new Territories.

" I do not wish to dwell on this branch of the subject at great length at this time, but allow me to repeat one thing that I have stated before. Brooks, the man who assaulted Senator Sumner on the floor of the Senate, and who was complimented with dinners and silver pitchers and gold-headed canes, and a good many other things for that feat, in one of his speeches declared that when this government was originally established, nobody expected that the institution of slavery would last until this day. That was but the opinion of one man, but it is such an opinion as we can never get from Judge Douglas or anybody in favour of slavery in the North at all. You can sometimes get it from a Southern man. He said at the same time that the framers of our government did not have the knowledge that experience has taught us — that experience and the invention of the cotton gin have taught us that the perpetuation of slavery is a necessity. He insisted therefore upon its being changed from the basis upon which the fathers of the government left it to the basis of perpetuation and nationalization.

"I insist that this is the difference between Judge Douglas and myself — that Judge Douglas is helping the change along. I insist upon this government being placed where our fathers originally placed it.

". . . When he asks me why we cannot get along with it [slavery] in the attitude where our fathers placed it, he had better clear up the evidences that he has himself changed it from that basis; that he has himself been chiefly instrumental in changing the policy of the fathers. Any one who will read his speech of the twenty-second of March last, will see that he there makes an open confession, showing that he set about fixing the institution upon an altogether different set of principles. . . .

" Now, fellow-citizens, in regard to this matter about a contract between myself and Judge Trumbull . . . I wish simply to say, what I have said to him before, that he cannot know whether it is true or not, and I do know that there is not a word of truth in it. And I have told him so before. I don't want any harsh language indulged in, but I do not know how to deal with this persistent insisting on a story that I know to be utterly without truth. It used to be the fashion amongst men that when a charge was made, some sort of proof was brought forward to establish it, and if no proof was found to exist it was dropped. I don't know how to meet this kind of an argument. I don't want to have a fight with Judge Douglas, and I have no way of making an argument up into the consistency of a corn-cob and stopping his mouth with it. All I can do is good-humouredly to say, that from the beginning to the end of all that story about a bargain between Judge Trumbull and myself, there is not a word of truth in it. . . .

" When that compromise [of 1850] was made, it did not repeal the old Missouri Compromise. It left a region of United States territory half as large as the present territory of the United States, north of the line of 36° 30′, in which slavery was prohibited by act of Congress. This compromise did not repeal that one. It did not affect nor propose to repeal it. But at last it became Judge Douglas's duty, as he thought (and I find no fault with him), as chairman of the Committee on Territories, to bring in a bill for the organisation of a territorial government — first of one, then of two Territories north of that line. When he did so, it ended in his inserting a provision substantially repealing the Missouri Compromise. That was because the Compromise of 1850 had not repealed it. And now I ask why he could not have left that compromise alone? We were quiet from the agitation of the slavery question. We were making no fuss about it. All had acquiesced in the compromise measures of 1850. We never had been seriously disturbed by any Abolition agitation before that period. . . . I close this part of the discussion on my part by asking him the question again, Why, when we had peace under the Missouri Compromise, could you not have let it alone?

" . . . He tries to persuade us that there must be a variety in the different institutions of the States of the Union; that that variety necessarily proceeds from the variety of soil, climate, of the face of the country, and the difference of the natural features of the States. I agree to all that. Have these very matters ever produced any difficulty amongst us? Not at all. Have we ever had any quarrel over the fact that they have laws in Louisiana designed to regulate the commerce that springs from the production of sugar, or because we have a different class relative to the production of flour in this State? Have they produced any differences? Not at all. They are the very cements of this Union. They don't make the house a house divided against itself. They are the props that hold up the house and sustain the Union.

But has it been so with this element of slavery? Have we not always had quarrels and difficulties over it? And when will we cease to have quarrels over it? Like causes produce like effects. It is worth while to observe that we have generally had comparative peace upon the slavery question, and that there has been no cause for alarm until it was excited by the effort to spread it into new territory. Whenever it has been limited to its present bounds, and there has been no effort to spread it, there has been peace. All the trouble and convulsion has proceeded from efforts to spread it over more territory. It was thus at the date of the Missouri Compromise. It was so again with the annexation of Texas; so with the territory acquired by the Mexican War; and it is so now. Whenever there has been an effort to spread it, there has been agitation and resistance. Now, I appeal to this audience (very few of whom are my political friends), as rational men, whether we have reason to expect that the agitation in regard to this subject will cease while the causes that tend to reproduce agitation are actively at work? Will not the same cause that produced agitation in 1820, when the Missouri Compromise was formed, — that which produced the agitation upon the annexation of Texas, and at other times, — work out the same results always? Do you think that the nature of man will be changed; that the same causes that produced agitation at one time will not have the same effect at another?

" This has been the result so far as my observation of the slavery question and my reading in history extend. What right have we then to hope that the trouble will cease, that the agitation will come to an end, until it shall either be placed back where it originally stood, and where the fathers originally placed it, or, on the other hand, until it shall entirely master all opposition? This is the view I entertain, and this is the reason why

I entertained it, as Judge Douglas has read from
my Springfield speech.

" . . . At Freeport I answered several interrogatories that had been propounded to me by Judge
Douglas at the Ottawa meeting. . . . At the same
time I propounded four interrogatories to him,
claiming it as a right that he should answer as
many for me as I did for him, and I would reserve myself for a future instalment when I got
them ready. The Judge, in answering me upon
that occasion, put in what I suppose he intends
as answers to all four of my interrogatories. The
first one of these I have before me, and it is in
these words : —

" *Question* 1. If the people of Kansas shall by means entirely unobjectionable in all other respects, adopt a State
constitution and ask admission into the Union under it,
before they have the requisite number of inhabitants according to the English bill — some 93,000 — will you vote
to admit them ?

" As I read the Judge's answer in the newspaper, and as I remember it as pronounced at
the time, he does not give any answer which is
equivalent to yes or no, — I will or I won't. He
answers at very considerable length, rather quar-
relling with me for asking the question, and insisting that Judge Trumbull had done something

that I ought to say something about; and finally, getting out such statements as induce me to infer that he means to be understood, he will, in that supposed case, vote for the admission of Kansas. I only bring this forward now, for the purpose of saying that, if he chooses to put a different construction upon his answer, he may do it. But if he does not, I shall from this time forward assume that he will vote for the admission of Kansas in disregard of the English bill. He has the right to remove any misunderstanding I may have. I only mention it now, that I may hereafter assume this to have been the true construction of his answer, if he does not now choose to correct me.

"The second interrogatory I propounded to him was this: —

"*Question* 2. Can the people of a United States Territory in any lawful way, against the wish of any citizen of the United States, exclude slavery from its limits prior to the formation of a State constitution?

"To this Judge Douglas answered that they can lawfully exclude slavery from the Territory prior to the formation of a constitution. He goes on to tell us how it can be done. As I understand him, he holds that it can be done by the territorial legislature refusing to make any enactments for the protection of slavery in the Territory, and especially by adopting unfriendly legislation to it. For the sake of clearness, I state it again : that they can exclude slavery from the Territory, — first, by withholding what he assumes to be an indispensable assistance to it in the way of legislation ; and second, by unfriendly legislation. If I rightly understand him, I wish to ask your attention for a while to his position.

"In the first place, the Supreme Court of the United States has decided that any congressional prohibition of slavery in the Territories is unconstitutional : they have reached this proposition as a conclusion from their former proposition that the Constitution of the United States expressly recognises property in slaves ; and from that other constitutional provision that no person shall be deprived of property without due process of law. Hence they reach the conclusion that as the Constitution of the United States expressly recognises property in slaves, and prohibits any person from being deprived of property without due process of law, to pass an act of Congress by which a man who owned a slave on one side of a line would be deprived of him if he took him on the other side, is depriving him of that property without due process of law. That I under-

stand to be the decision of the Supreme Court.
I understand also that Judge Douglas adheres
most firmly to that decision ; and the difficulty
is, how is it possible for any power to exclude
slavery from the Territory unless in violation of
that decision ? That is the difficulty.

"In the Senate of the United States, in 1856,
Judge Trumbull in a speech, substantially if not
directly, put the same interrogatory to Judge
Douglas, as to whether the people of a Territory
had the lawful power to exclude slavery prior to
the formation of a constitution ? Judge Douglas
then answered at considerable length, and his
answer will be found in the ' Congressional
Globe,' under date of June 9, 1856. The Judge
said that whether the people could exclude slavery prior to the formation of a constitution or
not, was a question to be decided by the Supreme
Court. He put that proposition, as will be seen
by the ' Congressional Globe,' in a variety of
forms, all running to the same thing in substance,
— that it was a question for the Supreme Court.
I maintain that when he says, after the Supreme
Court has decided the question, that the people
may yet exclude slavery by any means whatever,
he does virtually say that it is not a question for
the Supreme Court. He shifts his ground. I

appeal to you whether he did not say it was a question for the Supreme Court? Has not the Supreme Court decided that question? When he now says that the people may exclude slavery, does he not make it a question for the people? Does he not virtually shift his ground and say that it is not a question for the court, but for the people? This is a very simple proposition, — a very plain and naked one. It seems to me that there is no difficulty in deciding it. In a variety of ways he said that it was a question for the Supreme Court. He did not stop then to tell us that, whatever the Supreme Court decides, the people can by withholding necessary 'police regulations' keep slavery out. He did not make any such answer. I submit to you now, whether the new state of the case has not induced the Judge to sheer away from his original ground? Would not this be the impression of every fair-minded man?

" I hold that the proposition that slavery cannot enter a new country without police regulations is historically false. It is not true at all. I hold that the history of this country shows that the institution of slavery was originally planted upon this continent without these 'police regulations' which the Judge now thinks necessary for the actual establishment of it. Not only so, but is there not another fact, — how came this Dred Scott decision to be made? It was made upon the case of a negro being taken and actually held in slavery in Minnesota Territory, claiming his freedom because the act of Congress prohibited his being so held there. Will the Judge pretend that Dred Scott was not held there without police regulations? There is at least one matter of record as to his having been held in slavery in the Territory, not only without police regulations, but in the teeth of congressional legislation supposed to be valid at the time. This shows that there is vigour enough in slavery to plant itself in a new country, even against unfriendly legislation. It takes not only law, but the enforcement of law to keep it out. That is the history of this country upon the subject.

"I wish to ask one other question. It being understood that the Constitution of the United States guarantees property in slaves in the Territories, if there is any infringement of the right of that property, would not the United States courts, organised for the government of the Territory, apply such remedy as might be necessary in that case? It is a maxim held by the courts that there is no wrong without its remedy; and the courts have a remedy for whatever is acknowledged and treated as a wrong.

"Again : I will ask you, my friends, if you were elected members of the legislature, what would be the first thing you would have to do before entering upon your duties? Swear to support the Constitution of the United States. Suppose you believe as Judge Douglas does, that the Constitution of the United States guarantees to your neighbour the right to hold slaves in that Territory, — that they are his property, — how can you clear your oaths unless you give him such legislation as is necessary to enable him to enjoy that property? What do you understand by supporting the Constitution of a State or of the United States? Is it not to give such constitutional helps to the rights established by that Constitution as may be practically needed? Can you, if you swear to support the Constitution and believe that the Constitution establishes a right, clear your oath without giving it support? Do you support the Constitution if, knowing or believing there is a right established under it which needs specific legislation, you withhold that legislation? Do you not violate and disregard your oath? I can conceive of nothing plainer in the world. There can be nothing in the words 'support the Constitution,' if you may run counter to it by refusing support to any right established under the Constitution. And what I say here will hold with still more force against the Judge's doctrine of 'unfriendly legislation.' How could you, having sworn to support the Constitution, and believing that it guaranteed the right to hold slaves in the Territories, assist in legislation intended to defeat that right? That would be violating your own view of the Constitution. Not only so, but if you were to do so, how long would it take the courts to hold your votes unconstitutional and void? Not a moment.

" Lastly, I would ask, is not Congress itself under obligation to give legislative support to any right that is established under the United States Constitution? I repeat the question, is not Congress itself bound to give legislative support to any right that is established in the United States Constitution? A member of Congress swears to support the Constitution of the United States, and if he sees a right established by that Constitution which needs specific legislative protection, can he clear his oath without giving that protection? Let me ask you why many of us, who are opposed to slavery upon principle, give our acquiescence to a fugitive-slave law? Why do we hold ourselves under obligations to pass such a law, and abide by it when passed? Because the Constitution makes provision that the owners of slaves shall have the right to reclaim them. It gives the right to reclaim slaves; and that right is, as Judge Douglas says, a barren right, unless there is legislation that will enforce it.

"The mere declaration, 'No person held to service or labour in one State, under the laws thereof, escaping into another, shall, in consequence of any law or regulation therein, be discharged from such service or labour, but shall be delivered up on claim of the party to whom such service or labour may be due,' is powerless without specific legislation to enforce it. Now, on what ground would a member of Congress who is opposed to slavery in the abstract, vote for a fugitive law, as I would deem it my duty to do? Because there is a constitutional right which needs legislation to enforce it. And, although it is distasteful to me, I have sworn to support the Constitution; and, having so sworn, I cannot conceive that I do support it if I withhold from that right any necessary legislation to make it practical. And if that is true in regard to a fugitive-slave law, is the right to have fugitive slaves reclaimed any better fixed in the Constitution than the right to hold slaves in the Territories? For this decision is a just exposition of the Constitution, as Judge Douglas thinks. Is the one right any better than the other? If I wished to refuse to give legislative support to slave property in the Territories, if a member of Congress, I could not do it, holding the view that the Constitution establishes that right. If I did it at all, it would be because I deny that this decision properly construes the Constitution. But if I acknowledge with Judge Douglas that this decision properly construes the Constitution, I cannot conceive that I would be less than a perjured man if I should refuse in Congress to give such protection to that property as in its nature it needed. . . ."

FROM MR. LINCOLN'S REJOINDER TO JUDGE DOUGLAS AT CHARLESTOWN, ILLINOIS.

September 18, 1858.

"Judge Douglas has said to you that he has not been able to get from me an answer to the question whether I am in favour of negro citizenship. So far as I know, the Judge never asked me the question before. He shall have no occasion ever to ask it again, for I tell him very frankly that I am not in favour of negro citizenship. . . . Now my opinion is, that the different States have the power to make a negro a citizen under the Constitution of the United States, if they choose. The Dred Scott decision decides that they have not that power. If the State of Illinois had that power, I should be opposed to the exercise of it. . . .

" . . . Judge Douglas has told me that he heard my speeches north and my speeches south, . . . and there was a very different cast of sentiment in the speeches made at the different points. I will not charge upon Judge Douglas that he wilfully misrepresents me, but I call upon every fair-minded man to take these speeches and read them, and I dare him to point out any difference between my speeches north and south. While I am here, perhaps I ought to say a word, if I have the time, in regard to the latter portion of the Judge's speech, which was a sort of declamation in reference to my having said that I entertained the belief that this government would not endure, half slave and half free. I have said so, and I did not say it without what seemed to me good reasons. It perhaps would require more time than I have now to set forth those reasons in detail; but let me ask you a few questions. Have we ever had any peace on this slavery question?

When are we to have peace upon it if it is kept in the position it now occupies? How are we ever to have peace upon it? That is an important question. To be sure, if we will all stop and allow Judge Douglas and his friends to march on in their present career until they plant the institution all over the nation, here and wherever else our flag waves, and we acquiesce in it, there will be peace. But let me ask Judge Douglas how he is going to get the people to do that? They have been wrangling over this question for forty years. This was the cause of the agitation resulting in the Missouri Compromise; this produced the troubles at the annexation of Texas, in the acquisition of the territory acquired in the Mexican War. Again, this was the trouble quieted by the Compromise of 1850, when it was settled 'for ever,' as both the great political parties declared in their national conventions. That 'for ever' turned out to be just four years, when Judge Douglas himself reopened it.

"When is it likely to come to an end? He introduced the Nebraska Bill in 1854, to put another end to the slavery agitation. He promised that it would finish it all up immediately, and he has never made a speech since, until he got into a quarrel with the President about the Lecompton constitution, in which he has not declared that we are just at the end of the slavery agitation. But in one speech, I think last winter, he did say that he did n't quite see when the end of the slavery agitation would come. Now he tells us again that it is all over, and the people of Kansas have voted down the Lecompton constitution. How is it over? That was only one of the attempts to put an end to the slavery agitation, — one of these ' final settlements.' Is Kansas in the Union? Has she formed a constitution that she is likely to come in under? Is not the slavery agitation still an open question in that Territory? . . . If Kansas should sink to-day, and leave a great vacant space in the earth's surface, this vexed question would still be among us. I say, then, there is no way of putting an end to the slavery agitation amongst us, but to put it back upon the basis where our fathers placed it; no way but to keep it out of our new Territories, — to restrict it for ever to the old States where it now exists. Then the public mind will rest in the belief that it is in the course of ultimate extinction. That is one way of putting an end to the slavery agitation.

" The other way is for us to surrender, and let Judge Douglas and his friends have their way, and plant slavery over all the States." . . .

FROM MR. LINCOLN'S REPLY TO JUDGE DOUGLAS
AT GALESBURG, ILLINOIS.

October 7, 1858.

" . . . The Judge has alluded to the Declaration of Independence, and insisted that negroes are not included in that Declaration ; and that it is a slander on the framers of that instrument to suppose that negroes were meant therein ; and he asks you, Is it possible to believe that Mr. Jefferson, who penned that immortal paper, could have supposed himself applying the language of that instrument to the negro race, and yet held a portion of that race in slavery? Would he not at once have freed them? I only have to remark upon this part of his speech (and that too, very briefly, for I shall not detain myself or you upon that point for any great length of time), that I believe the entire records of the world, from the date of the Declaration of Independence up to within three years ago, may be searched in vain for one single affirmation from one single man, that the negro was not included in the Declaration of Independence ; I think I may defy Judge Douglas to show that he ever said so, that Washington ever said so, that any President ever said so, that any member of Congress ever said so, or that any living man upon the whole earth ever said so, until the necessities of the present policy of the Democratic party in regard to slavery had to invent that affirmation. And I will remind Judge Douglas and this audience, that while Mr. Jefferson was the owner of slaves, as undoubtedly he was, in speaking on this very subject, he used the strong language that 'he trembled for his country when he remembered that God was just;' and I will offer the highest premium in my power to Judge Douglas if he will show that he, in all his life, ever uttered a sentiment at all akin to that of Jefferson.

". . . In order to fix extreme Abolitionism upon me, Judge Douglas read a set of resolutions which he declared had been passed by a Republican State Convention, in October, 1854, held at Springfield, Illinois, and he declared that I had taken a part in that convention. It turned out that although a few men calling themselves an anti-Nebraska State Convention had sat at Springfield about that time, yet neither did I take any part in it, nor did it pass the resolutions or any such resolutions as Judge Douglas read. . . . A fraud, an absolute forgery, was committed, and the perpetration of it was traced to the three, — Lanphier, Harris, and Douglas. . . . The main object of that forgery at that time was to beat Yates and elect Harris to Congress, and that object was known to be exceedingly dear to Judge Douglas at that time.

" . . . The fraud having been apparently successful upon that occasion, both Harris and Douglas have more than once since then been attempting to put it to new uses. As the fisherman's wife, whose drowned husband was brought home with his body full of eels, said, when she was asked what was to be done with him, ' Take out the eels and set him again,' so Harris and Douglas have shown a disposition to take the eels out of that stale fraud by which they gained Harris's election, and set the fraud again, more than once. . . . And now that it has been discovered publicly to be a fraud, we find that Judge Douglas manifests no surprise at all. . . . But meanwhile the three are agreed that each is a most honourable man."

Mr. Lincoln's Reply to Judge Douglas in the
Seventh and Last Joint Debate at Alton,
Illinois.

October 15, 1858.

" . . . When have we had perfect peace in
regard to this thing [slavery] which I say is an
element of discord in this Union? We have
sometimes had peace, but when was it? It was
when the institution of slavery remained quiet
where it was. We have had difficulty and tur-
moil whenever it has made a struggle to spread
itself where it was not. I ask then, if experience
does not speak in thunder-tones, telling us that
the policy which has given peace to the country
heretofore, being returned to, gives the greatest
promise of peace again? You may say . . . that
all this difficulty in regard to the institution of
slavery is the mere agitation of office-seekers
and ambitious Northern politicians. . . . I agree
that there are office-seekers amongst us. The
Bible says somewhere that we are desperately
selfish. I think we would have discovered that
fact without the Bible. I do not claim that I
am any less so than the average of men, but I
do claim that I am not more selfish than Judge
Douglas.

" But is it true that all the difficulty and agitation we have in regard to this institution of slavery springs from office-seeking, — from the mere ambition of politicians? Is that the truth? How many times have we had danger from this question? Go back to the day of the Missouri Compromise. Go back to the nullification question, at the bottom of which lay this same slavery question. Go back to the time of the annexation of Texas. Go back to the troubles that led to the Compromise of 1850. You will find that every time, with the single exception of the nullification question, they sprung from an endeavour to spread this institution. There never was a party in the history of this country, and there probably never will be, of sufficient strength to disturb the general peace of the country. Parties themselves may be divided and quarrel on minor questions, yet it extends not beyond the parties themselves. But does not this question make a disturbance outside of political circles? Does it not enter into the churches and rend them asunder? What divided the great Methodist Church into two parts North and South? What has raised this constant disturbance in every Presbyterian General Assembly that meets? What disturbed the Unitarian Church in this very city two years ago?

What has jarred and shaken the great American Tract Society recently, — not yet splitting it, but sure to divide it in the end? Is it not this same mighty, deep-seated power, that somehow operates on the minds of men, exciting and stirring them up in every avenue of society, in politics, in religion, in literature, in morals, in all the manifold relations of life? Is this the work of politicians? Is that irresistible power which for fifty years has shaken the government and agitated the people, to be stilled and subdued by pretending that it is an exceedingly simple thing, and we ought not to talk about it? If you will get everybody else to stop talking about it, I assure you that I will quit before they have half done so. But where is the philosophy or statesmanship which assumes that you can quiet that disturbing element in our society, which has disturbed us for more than half a century, which has been the only serious danger that has threatened our institutions? I say where is the philosophy or the statesmanship, based on the assumption that we are to quit talking about it, and that the public mind is all at once to cease being agitated by it? Yet this is the policy here in the North that Douglas is advocating, — that we are to care nothing about it! I ask you if it is not a false philosophy? Is it not a false states-

manship that undertakes to build up a system of
policy upon the basis of caring nothing about the
very thing that everybody does care the most
about, — a thing which all experience has shown
we care about a very great deal?

" . . . The real issue in this controversy — the
one pressing upon every mind — is the sentiment
on the part of one class that looks upon the institution of slavery as a wrong, and of another class
that does not look upon it as a wrong. The sentiment that contemplates the institution of slavery
in this country as a wrong is the sentiment of the
Republican party. It is the sentiment around
which all their actions, all their arguments, circle ;
from which all their propositions radiate. They
look upon it as being a moral, social, and political
wrong ; and while they contemplate it as such,
they nevertheless have due regard for its actual
existence among us, and the difficulties of getting
rid of it in any satisfactory way, and to all the
constitutional obligations thrown about it. Yet,
having a due regard for these, they desire a policy
in regard to it that looks to its not creating any
more danger. They insist that it, as far as may
be, be treated as a wrong ; and one of the methods
of treating it as a wrong is to make provision that
it shall grow no larger. They also desire a policy

that looks to a peaceful end of slavery some time, as being a wrong. These are the views they entertain in regard to it, as I understand them ; and all their sentiments, all their arguments and propositions are brought within this range. I have said, and I here repeat it, that if there be a man amongst us who does not think that the institution of slavery is wrong in any one of the aspects of which I have spoken, he is misplaced, and ought not to be with us. And if there be a man amongst us who is so impatient of it as a wrong as to disregard its actual presence among us, and the difficulty of getting rid of it suddenly in a satisfactory way, and to disregard the constitutional obligations thrown about it, that man is misplaced if he is on our platform. We disclaim sympathy with him in practical action. He is not placed properly with us.

" On this subject of treating it as a wrong and limiting its spread, let me say a word. Has anything ever threatened the existence of this Union save and except this very institution of slavery? What is it that we hold most dear amongst us? Our own liberty and prosperity. What has ever threatened our liberty and prosperity save and except this institution of slavery? If this is true, how do you propose to improve the condition of

things by enlarging slavery, — by spreading it out
and making it bigger? You may have a wen or a
cancer upon your person, and not be able to cut
it out lest you bleed to death; but surely it is no
way to cure it, to engraft it and spread it over
your whole body. That is no proper way of
treating what you regard as a wrong. You see
this peaceful way of dealing with it as a wrong, —
restricting the spread of it, and not allowing it to
go into new countries where it has not already
existed. That is the peaceful way — the old-
fashioned way — the way in which the fathers
themselves set us the example.

"On the other hand, I have said there is a
sentiment which treats it as not being wrong.
That is the Democratic sentiment of this day.
I do not mean to say that every man who stands
within that range positively asserts that it is right.
That class will include all who positively assert
that it is right, and all who, like Judge Douglas,
treat it as indifferent, and do not say it is either
right or wrong. These two classes of men fall
within the general class of those who do not look
upon it as a wrong. And if there be among you
anybody who supposes that he, as a Democrat,
can consider himself ' as much opposed to slavery
as anybody,' I would like to reason with him.

12

You never treat it *as* a wrong. What other thing that you consider a wrong do you deal with as you deal with that? Perhaps you say it is wrong, but your leader never does, and you quarrel with anybody who says it is wrong. Although you pretend to say so yourself, you can find no fit place to deal with it as a wrong. You must not say anything about it in the free States, because it is not here. You must not say anything about it in the slave States, because it is there. You must not say anything about it in the pulpit, because that is religion, and has nothing to do with it. You must not say anything about it in politics, because that will disturb the security of ' my place.' There is no place to talk about it as being a wrong, although you say yourself it is a wrong. But, finally, you will screw yourself up to the belief that if the people of the slave States should adopt a system of gradual emancipation on the slavery question, you would be in favour of it. You would be in favour of it! You say that is getting it in the right place, and you would be glad to see it succeed. But you are deceiving yourself. You all know that Frank Blair and Gratz Brown, down there in St. Louis, undertook to introduce that system in Missouri. They fought as valiantly as they could for the system of gradual emancipation, which you pretend you would be glad to see succeed. Now I will bring you to the test. After a hard fight they were beaten; and when the news came over here, you threw up your hats and hurrahed for Democracy! More than that; take all the argument made in favour of the system you have proposed, and it carefully excludes the idea that there is anything wrong in the institution of slavery. The arguments to sustain that policy carefully exclude it. Even here to-day, you heard Judge Douglas quarrel with me, because I uttered a wish that it might sometime come to an end. Although Henry Clay could say he wished every slave in the United States was in the country of his ancestors, I am denounced by those who pretend to respect Henry Clay, for uttering a wish that it might sometime, in some peaceful way, come to an end.

"The Democratic policy in regard to that institution will not tolerate the merest breath, the slightest hint, of the least degree of wrong about it. Try it by some of Judge Douglas's arguments. He says he 'don't care whether it is voted up or voted down.' . . . Any man can say that who does not see anything wrong in slavery. . . . But if it is a wrong, he cannot say that people have a right to do wrong. He says that, upon the score of equality, slaves should be allowed to go into a new Territory like other property. This is strictly logical if there is no difference between it and other property. . . . But if you insist that one is wrong and the other right, there is no use to institute a comparison between right and wrong. . . . The Democratic policy everywhere carefully excludes the idea that there is anything wrong in it.

"That is the real issue. That is the issue that will continue in this country when these poor tongues of Judge Douglas and myself shall be silent. It is the eternal struggle between these two principles — right and wrong — throughout the world. They are the two principles that have stood face to face from the beginning of time, and will ever continue to struggle. The one is the common right of humanity, and the other the divine right of kings. It is the same principle in whatever shape it develops itself. It is the same spirit that says, 'You toil and work and earn bread, and I 'll eat it.' No matter in what shape it comes, whether from the mouth of a king, who seeks to bestride the people of his own nation and live by the fruit of their labour, or from one race of men as an apology for enslaving another

race, — it is the same tyrannical principle. . . .
Whenever the issue can be distinctly made, and
all extraneous matter thrown out, so that men can
fairly see the real difference between the parties,
this controversy will soon be settled, and it will
be done peaceably, too. There will be no war,
no violence. It will be placed again where the
wisest and best men of the world placed it. . . .
I now say that, willingly or unwillingly, purposely
or without purpose, Judge Douglas has been the
most prominent instrument in changing the position of the institution of slavery, which the fathers
of the government .expected to come to an end
ere this, . . . and placing it where he openly con-
fesses he has no desire there shall ever be an
end to it."

From his Speech at Columbus, Ohio.

September 16, 1859.

". . . The American people, on the first day
of January, 1854, found the African slave-trade
prohibited by a law of Congress. In a majority
of the States of this Union, they found African
slavery, or any other sort of slavery, prohibited
by State constitutions. They also found a law
existing, supposed to be valid, by which slavery

was excluded from almost all the territory the
United States then owned. This was the condition of the country with reference to the institution of slavery, on the 1st of January, 1854.
A few days after that, a bill was introduced into
Congress, which ran through its regular course in
the two branches of the national legislature, and
finally passed into a law in the month of May,
by which the Act of Congress prohibiting slavery
from going into the Territories of the United
States was repealed. In connection with the law
itself, and, in fact, in the terms of the law, the
then existing prohibition was not only repealed,
but there was a declaration of a purpose on the
part of Congress never thereafter to exercise any
power that they might have, real or supposed, to
prohibit the extension or the spread of slavery.
This was a very great change, for the law thus
repealed was of more than thirty years' standing.
Following rapidly upon the heels of this action
of Congress, a decision of the Supreme Court is
made, by which it is declared that Congress, if it
desires to prohibit the spread of slavery, has
no constitutional power to do so. . . . That decision lays down principles which, if pushed to
their logical conclusion, — I say pushed to their
logical conclusion, — would decide that the con-

stitutions of free States forbidding slavery were themselves unconstitutional.

" . . . The Republican party, as I understand its principles and policy, believes that there is great danger of the institution of slavery being spread out and extended, until it is ultimately made alike lawful in all the States of this Union; so believing, to prevent that incidental and ultimate consummation is the original and chief purpose of the Republican organisation.

" . . . The chief danger to this purpose is . . . that insidious Douglas popular-sovereignty. This is the miner and sapper. While it does not propose to revive the African slave-trade, nor to pass a slave-code, nor to make a second Dred Scott decision, it is preparing us for the onslaught and charge of these ultimate enemies when they shall be ready to come on, and the word of command for them to advance shall be given. I say this *Douglas* popular-sovereignty — for there is a broad distinction, as I now understand it, between that article and a genuine popular-sovereignty.

" I believe there is a genuine popular-sovereignty. I think a definition of genuine popular-sovereignty in the abstract would be about this: that each man shall do precisely as he pleases with himself, and ᵗʰ all those things which exclusively concern him. Applied to governments, this principle would be, that a general government shall do all those things which pertain to it; and all the local governments shall do precisely as they please in respect to those matters which exclusively concern them. I understand that this government of the United States under which we live, is based upon this principle; and I am misunderstood if it is supposed that I have any war to make upon that principle.

"Now, what is Judge Douglas's popular-sovereignty? It is, as a principle, no other than that if one man chooses to make a slave of another man, neither that other man nor anybody else has a right to object. Applied in government, as he seeks to apply it, it is this: If, in a new Territory into which a few people are beginning to enter for the purpose of making their homes, they choose to either exclude slavery from their limits or to establish it there, however one or the other may affect the persons to be enslaved, or the infinitely greater number of persons who are afterward to inhabit that Territory, or the other members of the families of communities of which they are but an incipient member, or the general head of the family of States as parent of all, — however their action may affect one or the other of these, there is no power or right to interfere. That is Douglas popular-sovereignty applied.

" He has a good deal of trouble with popular sovereignty. His explanations explanatory of explanations explained are interminable. The most lengthy and, as I suppose, the most maturely considered of his long series of explanations is his great essay in ' Harper's Magazine.' . . . In that article he quotes from two persons belonging to the Republican party, without naming them, but who can readily be recognised as being Governor Seward of New York and myself. . . .

" . . . The sense of that quotation condensed, is this : that this slavery element is a durable element of discord among us, and that we shall probably not have perfect peace in this country with it until it either masters the free principle in our government, or is so far mastered by the free principle as for the public mind to rest in the belief that it is going to its end. . . . Judge Douglas has been so much annoyed by the expression of that sentiment that he has constantly, I believe, in almost all his speeches since it was uttered, been referring to it. . . . I only ask your attention to this matter for the purpose of making one or two points upon it.

" . . . Judge Douglas himself says in his ' copyright essay,' that a controversy between the American colonies and the government of Great Britain began on the slavery question in 1699, and continued from that time until the Revolution ; and while he did not say so, we all know that it has continued with more or less violence ever since the Revolution. . . . Then we know from Judge Douglas himself, that slavery began to be an element of discord among the white people of this country as far back as 1699, or one hundred and sixty years ago, or five generations of men, counting thirty years to a generation.   Now it would seem to me that it might have occurred to Judge Douglas, or to anybody who had turned his attention to these facts, that there was something in the nature of that thing — slavery — somewhat durable for mischief and discord.

" . . . From the adoption of the Constitution down to 1820, is the precise period of our history when we had comparative peace upon this question, — the precise period of time when we came nearer to having peace about it than any other time of that entire one hundred and sixty years in which he says it began, or of the eighty years of our own Constitution. . . . This was the precise period of time in which our fathers adopted,

and during which they followed, a policy restricting the spread of slavery, and the whole Union
was acquiescing in it. The whole country looked
forward to the ultimate extinction of the institution. It was when a policy had been adopted
and was prevailing, which led all just and right-
minded men to suppose that slavery was gradually
coming to an end, and that they might be quiet
about it, watching it as it expired. I think Judge
Douglas might have perceived that too; and,
whether he did or not, it is worth the attention
of fair-minded men, here and elsewhere, to consider whether that is not the truth of the case.
If he had looked at these two facts, . . . he
might then, perhaps, have been brought to a
more just appreciation of what I said fifteen
months ago, that 'a house divided against itself
cannot stand.' . . . In connection with it I said,
' we are now far advanced into the fifth year since
a policy was initiated with the avowed object and
confident promise of putting an end to slavery
agitation. Under the operation of that policy,
that agitation has not only not ceased, but has
constantly augmented.' I now say to you here,
that we are advanced still farther into the sixth
year since that policy of Judge Douglas — that
popular sovereignty of his for quieting the slavery

question — was made the national policy. Fifteen months more have been added since I uttered that sentiment, and I call upon you and all other right-minded men, to say whether those fifteen months have belied or corroborated my words.

". . . I cannot but express my gratitude that this true view of this element of discord among us, as I believe it is, is attracting more and more attention. I do not believe that Governor Seward uttered that sentiment because I had done so before, but because he reflected upon this subject, and saw the truth of it. Nor do I believe, because Governor Seward or I uttered it, that Mr. Hickman of Pennsylvania, in different language, since that time, has declared his belief in the utter antagonism which exists between the principles of liberty and slavery. You see we are multiplying. Now, while I am speaking of Hickman, let me say, I know but little about him. I have never seen him, and know scarcely anything about the man; but I will say this much about him: of all the anti-Lecompton Democracy that have been brought to my notice, he alone has the true, genuine ring of the metal.

". . . Judge Douglas . . . proceeds to assume, without proving it, that slavery is one of those little, unimportant, trivial matters which are of just about as much consequence as the question would be to me, whether my neighbour should raise horned cattle or plant tobacco ; that there is no moral question about it, but that it is altogether a matter of dollars and cents ; that when a new Territory is opened for settlement, the first man who goes into it may plant there a thing which, like the Canada thistle or some other of those pests of the soil, cannot be dug out by the millions of men who will come thereafter ; that it is one of those little things that is so trivial in its nature that it has no effect upon anybody save the few men who first plant upon the soil ; that it is not a thing which in any way affects the family of communities composing these States, nor any way endangers the general government. Judge Douglas ignores altogether the very well-known fact that we have never had a serious menace to our political existence except it sprang from this thing, which he chooses to regard as only upon a par with onions and potatoes.

" . . . This is an idea, I suppose, which has arisen in Judge Douglas's mind from his peculiar structure. I suppose the institution of slavery really looks small to him. He is so put up by nature that a lash upon his back would hurt him, but a lash upon anybody else's back does not hurt him. That is the build of the man, and consequently he looks upon the matter of slavery in this unimportant light.

" Judge Douglas ought to remember, when he is endeavouring to force this policy upon the American people, that while he is put up in that way, a good many are not. He ought to remember . . . Thomas Jefferson, . . . who was led to exclaim, ' I tremble for my country when I remember that God is just.' . . . There was danger to this country, danger of the avenging justice of God, in that little, unimportant popular-sovereignty question of Judge Douglas. He supposed there was a question of God's eternal justice wrapped up in the enslaving of any race of men, or any man, and that those who did so braved the arm of Jehovah, — that when a nation thus dared the Almighty, every friend of that nation had cause to dread His wrath. Choose ye between Jefferson and Douglas as to what is the true view of this element among us.

" . . . Now, if you are opposed to slavery honestly, I ask you to note that fact (the popular-sovereignty of Judge Douglas), and the like of which is to follow, to be plastered on, layer after layer, until very soon you are prepared to deal with the negro everywhere as with the brute. If

public sentiment has not been debauched already
to this point, a new turn of the screw in that
direction is all that is wanting; and this is constantly being done by the teachers of this insidious popular-sovereignty. You need but one or
two turns further, until your minds, now ripening
under these teachings, will be ready for all these
things, and you will receive and support or submit to the slave-trade, revived with all its horrors,
— a slave-code enforced in our Territories, —
and a new Dred Scott decision to bring slavery
up into the very heart of the free North.

" . . . I ask attention to the fact that in a pre-
eminent degree these popular sovereigns are at
this work: blowing out the moral lights around
us; teaching that the negro is no longer a man,
but a brute; that the Declaration has nothing to
do with him; that he ranks with the crocodile
and the reptile; that man with body and soul is
a matter of dollars and cents. I suggest to this
portion of the Ohio Republicans, or Democrats,
if there be any present, the serious consideration
of this fact, that there is now going on among
you a steady process of debauching public opinion on this subject. With this, my friends, I bid
you adieu."

From his Speech at Cincinnati, Ohio.

September 17, 1859.

" . . . I am what they call, as I understand it, a 'Black Republican.' I think slavery is wrong, morally and politically. I desire that it should be no further spread in these United States, and I should not object if it should gradually terminate in the whole Union. While I say this for myself, I say to you, Kentuckians, that I understand you differ radically with me upon this proposition; that you believe slavery is a good thing; that slavery is right; that it ought to be extended and perpetuated in this Union. Now, there being this broad difference between us, I do not pretend, in addressing myself to you, Kentuckians, to attempt proselyting you. That would be a vain effort. I do not enter upon it. I only propose to try to show you that you ought to nominate for the next presidency, at Charleston, my distinguished friend, Judge Douglas. In all that, there is no real difference between you and him; I understand he is as sincerely for you, and more wisely for you than you are for yourselves. I will try to demonstrate that proposition.

" . . . What do you want more than anything else to make successful your views of slavery, — to advance the outspread of it, and to secure and perpetuate the nationality of it? What do you want more than anything else? What is needed absolutely? What is indispensable to you? Why, if I may be allowed to answer the question, it is to retain a hold upon the North; to retain support and strength from the free States. If you can get this support and strength from the free States, you can succeed. If you do not get this support and this strength from the free States, you are in a minority, and you are beaten at once.

" If that proposition be admitted, and it is undeniable, then the next thing I say to you is, that Douglas, of all men in this nation, is the only man that affords you any hold upon the free States; that no other man can give you any strength in the free States. This being so, if you doubt the other branch of the proposition, whether he is really for you, as I have expressed it, I propose asking your attention for a while to a few facts.

" . . . In the first place, we know that, in a government like this, — a government of the people, where the voice of all the men of the country, substantially, enters into the administration of the government, — what lies at the bottom of all of it, is public opinion. I lay down the proposition that Judge Douglas is not only the man

13

that promises you in advance a hold upon the
North, and support in the North, but that he
constantly moulds public opinion to your ends;
that in every possible way he can, he moulds the
public opinion of the North to your ends; and if
there are a few things in which he seems to be
against you, — a few things which he says that
appear to be against you; and a few things that
he forbears to say, which you would like to have
him say, — you ought to remember that the saying
of the one, or the forbearing to say the other,
would lose his hold upon the North, and by consequence would lose his capacity to serve you.

" Upon this subject of moulding public opinion,
I call your attention to the fact — for a well-
established fact it is — that the Judge never says
your institution of slavery is wrong; he never
says it is right, to be sure, but he never says it is
wrong.   There is not a public man in the United
States, I believe, with the exception of Senator
Douglas, who has not, at some time in his life,
declared his opinion whether the thing is right or
wrong; but Senator Douglas never declares it is
wrong.   He leaves himself at perfect liberty to
do all in your favour which he would be hindered
from doing if he were to declare the thing to be
wrong.   On the contrary, he takes all the chances

that he has for inveigling the sentiment of the North, opposed to slavery, into your support, by never saying it is right. This you ought to set down to his credit. You ought to give him full credit for this much, little though it be in comparison with the whole which he does for you.

" Some other things I will ask your attention to. He said upon the floor of the Senate of the United States, and he has repeated it, as I understand, a great many times, that he does not care ' whether slavery is voted up or voted down.' This again shows you, or ought to show you, if you would reason upon it, that he does not believe it to be wrong ; for a man may say, when he sees nothing wrong in a thing, that he does not care whether it be voted up or voted down ; but no man can logically say that he cares not whether a thing goes up or down which appears to him to be wrong. You therefore have a demonstration in this, that to Judge Douglas's mind, your favourite institution, which you desire to have spread out and made perpetual, is no wrong

" Another thing he tells you in a speech made in Memphis . . . last year. He there distinctly told the people that there was ' a line drawn by the Almighty across this continent,' on one side of which ' the soil must always be cultivated by

slaves; ' that he did not pretend to know exactly
where that line was, but there was such a line.
I want to ask your attention to that proposition
again : that there is one portion of this continent
where the Almighty has designed the soil shall
always be cultivated by slaves ; that its being cultivated by slaves at that place is right ; that it has
the direct sympathy and authority of the Almighty.
Whenever you can get these Northern audiences
to adopt the opinion that slavery is right on the
other side of the Ohio ; whenever you can get
them, in pursuance of Douglas's views, to adopt
that sentiment, — they will very readily make the
other argument, which is perfectly logical, that
that which is right on that side of the Ohio cannot be wrong on this, and that if you have that
property on that side of the Ohio, under the seal
and stamp of the Almighty, when by any means
it escapes over here, it is wrong to have constitutions and laws to ' devil ' you about it.

". . . Let me ask your attention to another
thing. . . . Five years ago no living man had
expressed the opinion that the negro had no
share in the Declaration of Independence. . . .
Within that space of five years Senator Douglas,
in the argument of this question, has got his
entire party . . . to join in saying that the negro

has no share in that Declaration of Independence. If there be now in all these United States one Douglas man that does not say this, I have been unable upon any occasion to scare him up. Now, if none of you said this five years ago, and all of you say it now, that is a vast change which you Kentuckians ought to note. . . . That change in public sentiment has already degraded the black man in the estimation of Douglas and his followers from the condition of a man of some sort, and assigned him to the condition of a brute.

" . . . In Kentucky perhaps — in many of the slave States certainly — . . . you are trying to show that slavery existed in the Bible times by Divine ordinance. Now, Douglas is wiser than you, for your own benefit, upon that subject. Douglas knows that whenever you establish that slavery was right by the Bible, it will occur that that slavery was the slavery of the white man, — of men without reference to colour, — and he knows very well that you may entertain that idea in Kentucky as much as you please, but you will never win any Northern support upon it. He makes a wiser argument for you. He makes the argument that the slavery of the black man — the slavery of the man who has a skin of a different colour from your own — is right. He thereby brings to your support

Northern voters, who could not for a moment be brought by your own argument of the Bible right of slavery.

" . . . At Memphis he [Judge Douglas] declared that in all contests between the negro and the white man, he was for the white man, but that in all questions between the negro and the crocodile, he was for the negro. . . .

" The first inference seems to be that if you do not enslave the negro, you are wronging the white man in some way or other ; and that whoever is opposed to the negro being enslaved is in some way or other against the white man. Is not that a falsehood? If there was a necessary conflict between the white man and the negro, I should be for the white man as much as Judge Douglas ; but I say there is no such necessary conflict. I say there is room enough for us all to be free, and that it not only does not wrong the white man that the negro should be free, but it positively wrongs the mass of the white men that the negro should be enslaved, — that the mass of white men are really injured by the effects of slave labour in the vicinity of the fields of their own labour. . . .

" There is one other thing that I will say to you in this relation. It is but my opinion ; I give it to you without a fee. It is my opinion

that it is for you to take him or be defeated ; and
that if you do take him you may be beaten. You
will surely be beaten if you do not take him.
We, the Republicans and others forming the opposition of the country, intend ' to stand by our
guns,' to be patient and firm, and in the long run
to beat you, whether you take him or not. We
know that before we fairly beat you, we have
to beat you both together. We know that ' you
are all of a feather,' and that we have to beat you
all together ; and we expect to do it. We don't
intend to be very impatient about it. We mean
to be as deliberate and calm about it as it is
possible to be, but as firm and resolved as it is
possible for men to be. When we do, as we say,
beat you, you perhaps want to know what we will
do with you.

" I will tell you, so far as I am authorised to speak
for the opposition, what we mean to do with you.
We mean to treat you as near as we possibly can
as Washington, Jefferson, and Madison treated
you. We mean to leave you alone, and in no
way to interfere with your institution ; to abide
by all and every compromise of the Constitution ;
and, in a word, coming back to the original proposition, to treat you, so far as degenerate men (if
we have degenerated) may, according to the ex-

ample of those noble fathers, Washington, Jefferson, and Madison. We mean to remember that you are as good as we; that there is no difference between us other than the difference of circumstances. We mean to recognise and bear in mind always, that you have as good hearts in your bosoms as other people, or as we claim to have, and to treat you accordingly. We mean to marry your girls when we have a chance — the white ones I mean; and I have the honour to say that I once did have a chance in that way.

"I have told you what we mean to do. I want to know, now, when that thing takes place, what do you mean to do? I often hear it intimated that you mean to divide the Union whenever a Republican, or anything like it, is elected President of the United States. Well, then, I want to know what you are going to do with your half of it? Are you going to split the Ohio down through, and push your half off a piece? Or are you going to keep it right alongside of us outrageous fellows? Or are you going to build up a wall some way between your country and ours, by which that movable property of yours can't come over here any more, to the danger of your losing it? Do you think you can better yourselves on that subject by leaving us here under no obligation whatever to return these specimens of your movable property that come hither? You have divided the Union because we would not do right with you, as you think, upon that subject. When we cease to be under obligation to do anything for you, how much better off do you think you will be? Why, gentlemen, I think you are as gallant and brave men as live; that you can fight as bravely in a good cause, man for man, as any other people living; that you have shown yourselves capable of this upon various occasions: but man for man you are not better than we are, and there are not so many of you as there are of us. You will never make much of a hand at whipping us. If we were fewer in numbers than you, I think you could whip us; if we were equal, it would likely be a drawn battle; but being inferior in numbers, you will make nothing by attempting to master us. . . .

.   .   .   .

" Labour is the great source from which nearly all, if not all, human comforts and necessities are drawn. There is a difference in opinion about the elements of labour in society. Some men assume that there is a necessary connection between capital and labour, and that connection draws within it the whole of the labour of the community. They assume that nobody works unless capital excites them to work. They begin next to consider what is the best way. They say there are but two ways, — one is to hire men and to allure them to labour by their consent ; the other is to buy the men, and drive them to it, and that is slavery. Having assumed that, they proceed to discuss the question of whether the labourers themselves are better off in the condition of slaves or of hired labourers, and they usually decide that they are better off in the condition of slaves.

" In the first place I say, the whole thing is a mistake. That there is a certain relation between capital and labour, I admit. That it does exist, and rightfully exist, I think is true. That men who are industrious and sober and honest in the pursuit of their own interests should after a while accumulate capital, and after that should be allowed to enjoy it in peace, and also if they should choose, when they have accumulated it, to use it to save themselves from actual labour, and hire other people to labour for them, — is right. In doing so, they do not wrong the man they employ, for they find men who have not their own land to work upon, or shops to work in, and who are benefited by working for others, — hired labourers, receiving their capital for it. Thus a few men that own capital hire a few others, and these establish the relation of capital and labour rightfully — a relation of which I make no complaint. But I insist that that relation, after all, does not embrace more than one eighth of the labour of the country.

" . . . I have taken upon myself . . . to say that upon these principles all expect ultimately to win. In order to do so, I think we want and must have a national policy in regard to the institution of slavery that acknowledges and deals with that institution as being wrong.

" Whoever desires the prevention of the spread of slavery and the nationalization of that institution, yields all when he yields to any policy that either recognises slavery as being right, or as being an indifferent thing. Nothing will make you successful but setting up a policy which shall treat the thing as being wrong. . . . We believe that the spreading out and perpetuity of the institution of slavery impairs the general welfare. We believe, nay, we know, that that is the only thing that has ever threatened the perpetuity of the Union itself. The only thing which has ever menaced the destruction of the government under which we live is this very thing. To repress this thing, we think is providing for the general welfare. . . .

. . . . . . , . .

" . . . There are a plenty of men in the slave States that are altogether good enough for me, to be either President or Vice-President, provided they will profess their sympathy with our purpose, and will place themselves on such ground that our men upon principle can vote for them. There are scores of them — good men in their character for intelligence, for talent and integrity. If such an one will place himself upon the right ground, I am for his occupying one place upon the next Republican or opposition ticket. I will go heartily for him. But unless he does so place himself, I think it is perfect nonsense to attempt to bring about a union upon any other basis; that if a union be made, the elements will so scatter that there can be no success for such a ticket. The good old maxims of the Bible are applicable, and truly applicable, to human affairs; and in this, as in other things, we may say that he who is not for us is against us; he who gathereth not with us, scattereth. I should be glad to have some of the many good and able and noble men of the South place themselves where we can confer upon them the high honour of an election upon

one or the other end of our ticket. It would
do my soul good to do that thing. It would enable us to teach them that inasmuch as we select
one of their own number to carry out our principles, we are free from the charge that we mean
more than we say."

FROM HIS SPEECH OF FEBRUARY 27, 1860, AT THE
COOPER INSTITUTE, NEW YORK.

[NOTE. — In this speech Mr. Lincoln maintained the negative of a question upon which
the Douglas Democrats held the affirmative, viz.,
Whether there was anything in the Constitution
which forbade the Federal government to control
slavery in the Territories of the United States?
After clearly showing that the thirty-nine members of the convention who signed the Constitution, and the seventy-six members of the Congress
which framed the amendments to it, also held the
negative of this question, he dealt with the threats
of the South to disrupt the Union if a Republican
President was elected, and the duty of loyal citizens to defend and maintain it. He said] :

" It is surely safe to assume that the thirty-
nine framers of the original Constitution, and
the seventy-six members of the Congress which
framed the amendments thereto, taken together,

do certainly include those who may be fairly called ' our fathers who framed the government under which we live.' And so assuming, I defy any man to show that any one of them ever, in his whole life, declared that, in his understanding, any proper division of local from Federal authority, or any part of the Constitution, forbade the Federal government to control as to slavery in the Federal Territories. I go a step further. I defy any one to show that any living man in the whole world ever did, prior to the beginning of the present century (and I might almost say, prior to the beginning of the last half of the present century), declare that, in his understanding, any proper division of local from Federal authority, or any part of the Constitution, forbade the Federal government to control as to slavery in the Federal Territories. To those who now so declare, I give not only ' our fathers who framed the government under which we live,' but with them all other living men within the century in which it was framed, among whom to search, and they shall not be able to find the evidence of a single man agreeing with them.

· · · · · · · ·

" But enough ! Let all who believe that ' our fathers who framed the government under which we live understood this question just as well, and even better than we do now,' speak as they spoke, and act as they acted upon it. This is all Republicans ask, all Republicans desire, in relation to slavery. As those fathers marked it, so let it again be marked, as an evil not to be extended, but to be tolerated and protected only because of and so far as its actual presence among us makes that toleration and protection a necessity. Let all the guaranties those fathers gave it be not grudgingly, but fully and fairly maintained. For this Republicans contend, and with this, so far as I know or believe, they will be content.

"And now, if they would listen, as I suppose they will not, I would address a few words to the Southern people.

"I would say to them : You consider yourselves a reasonable and a just people ; and I consider that in the general qualities of reason and justice you are not inferior to any other people. Still, when you speak of us Republicans, you do so only to denounce us as reptiles, or, at the best, as no better than outlaws. You will grant a hearing to pirates or murderers, but nothing like it to ' Black Republicans.' In all your contentions with one another, each of you deems an unconditional condemnation of ' Black Republicanism ' as the first thing to be attended to. Indeed, such condemnation of us seems to be an indispensable prerequisite, licence, so to speak, among you, to be admitted or permitted to speak at all. Now, can you or not be prevailed upon to pause and to consider whether this is quite just to us, or even to yourselves? Bring forward your charges and specifications, and then be patient long enough to hear us deny or justify.

" You say we are sectional. We deny it. That makes an issue ; and the burden of proof is upon you. You produce your proof, and what is it? Why, that our party has no existence in your section — gets no votes in your section. The fact is substantially true ; but does it prove the issue? If it does, then in case we should, without change of principle, begin to get votes in your section, we should thereby cease to be sectional. You cannot escape this conclusion ; and yet, are you willing to abide by it? If you are, you will probably soon find that we have ceased to be sectional, for we shall get votes in your section this very year. . . . The fact that we get no votes in your section, is a fact of your making and not of ours. And if there be fault in that fact, that fault is primarily yours, and remains so until you show that we repel you by some wrong principle or practice. If we do repel you by any

wrong principle or practice, the fault is ours ;
but this brings you to where you ought to have
started, — to a discussion of the right or wrong
of our principle. If our principle, put in practice, would wrong your section for the benefit of
ours, or for any other object, then our principle
and we with it are sectional, and are justly opposed and denounced as such. Meet us, then,
on the question of whether our principle, put in
practice, would wrong your section, and so meet
us as if it were possible that something may be
said on our side. Do you accept the challenge?
No ! Then you really believe that the principle
which ' our fathers who framed the government
under which we live ' thought so clearly right as
to adopt it, and indorse it again and again upon
their official oaths, is, in fact, so clearly wrong as
to demand your condemnation without a moment's
consideration.

" Some of you delight to flaunt in our faces the
warning against sectional parties given by Washington in his Farewell Address. Less than eight
years before Washington gave that warning, he
had, as President of the United States, approved
and signed an act of Congress enforcing the prohibition of slavery in the Northwestern Territory ;
. . . and about one year after he penned it [that

14

warning] he wrote Lafayette that he considered that prohibition a wise measure, expressing in the same connection his hope that we should at some time have a confederacy of free States. . . .

"Again, you say we have made the slavery question more prominent than it formerly was. We deny it. . . . It was not we but you who discarded the old policy of the fathers. We resisted, and still resist, your innovation; and thence comes the greater prominence of the question. Would you have that question reduced to its former proportions? Go back to that old policy. . . . If you would have the peace of the old times, re-adopt the precepts and policy of the old times.

"You charge that we stir up insurrections among your slaves. We deny it; and what is your proof? Harper's Ferry? John Brown? John Brown was no Republican; and you have failed to implicate a single Republican in his Harper's Ferry enterprise. If any member of our party is guilty in that matter, you know it, or you do not know it. If you do know it, you are inexcusable for not designating the man and proving the fact. If you do not know it, you are inexcusable for asserting it. . . .

". . . John Brown's effort was peculiar. It was not a slave insurrection. It was an attempt by white men to get up a revolt among slaves, in which the slaves refused to participate. In fact, it was so absurd that the slaves, with all their ignorance, saw plainly enough it could not succeed. That affair, in its philosophy, corresponds with the many attempts . . . at the assassination of kings and emperors. An enthusiast . . . ventures the attempt, . . . which ends in little else than his own execution. . . .

. . . .

" . . . But you will not abide the election of a Republican president ! In that supposed event, you say you will destroy the Union ; and then you say the great crime of having destroyed it will be upon us ! That is cool. A highwayman holds a pistol to my ear, and mutters through his teeth, 'Stand and deliver, or I shall kill you, and then you will be a murderer !'

. . . .

" If slavery is right, all words, acts, laws, and constitutions against it are themselves wrong, and should be silenced and swept away. If it is right, we cannot justly object to its nationality — its universality ; if it is wrong, they cannot justly insist upon its extension — its enlargement. All they ask we could readily grant, if we thought slavery right ; all we ask they could as readily grant if they thought it wrong. Their thinking it right and our thinking it wrong, is the precise fact upon which depends the whole controversy. Thinking it right, as they do, they are not to blame for desiring its full recognition as being right; but thinking it wrong, as we do, can we yield to them? Can we cast our votes with their view, and against our own? In view of our moral, social, and political responsibilities, can we do this?

"Wrong as we think slavery is, we can yet afford to let it alone where it is, because that much is due to the necessity arising from its actual presence in the nation; but can we, while our votes will prevent it, allow it to spread into the national Territories, and to overrun us here in these free States? If our sense of duty forbids this, then let us stand by our duty fearlessly and effectively. Let us be diverted by none of those sophistical contrivances wherewith we are so industriously plied and belaboured, — contrivances such as groping for some middle ground between the right and the wrong, vain as the search for a man who should be neither a living man nor a dead man; such as a policy of 'don't care,' on a question about which all true men do care; such as Union appeals beseeching true Union men to yield to disunionists, reversing the Divine rule, and calling not the sinners, but the righteous to repentance ; such as invocations to Washington, imploring men to unsay what Washington said, and undo what Washington did.

"Neither let us be slandered from our duty by false accusations against us, nor frightened from it by menaces of destruction to the government, nor of dungeons to ourselves. Let us have faith that right makes might, and in that faith let us to the end dare to do our duty as we understand it."

From his Speech at New Haven, Connecticut.

March 6, 1860.

[Note. — This speech was in large part a repetition of his speech at the Cooper Institute in New York on the 27th of February, 1860, the phraseology being slightly changed in some paragraphs and unchanged in others. One of his illustrations of the right of the people of the free States — while leaving slavery alone in the slave States — to prevent its extension, was new and forcible. After stating that the Tariff, the National Domain, and other subjects of national interest would not receive attention while the question of the extension of slavery remained open, he asked :]

" . . . What ever endangered this Union save
and except slavery? Did any other thing ever
cause a moment's fear? All men must agree that
this thing alone has ever endangered the perpetuity of the Union. But if it was ever threatened by any other influence, would not all men
say that the best thing that could be done, if we
could not or ought not to destroy it, would be at
least to keep it from growing any larger? Can
any man believe that the way to save the Union
is to extend and increase the only thing that
threatens the Union, and to suffer it to grow
bigger and bigger?

" . . . There are but two policies in regard to
slavery that can be at all maintained. The first,
based on the property view, that slavery is right,
conforms to that idea throughout, and demands
that we should do everything for it that we ought
to do if it were right. . . .

" . . . The other policy is one that squares
with the idea that slavery is wrong, and it consists in doing everything that we ought to do if
it is wrong. Now I don't wish to be misunderstood, nor to leave a gap down, to be misrepresented, even. I don't mean that we ought to
attack it where it exists. To me it seems that
if we were to form a government anew, in view

of the actual presence of slavery, we should find it necessary to frame just such a government as our fathers did, — giving to the slaveholder the entire control where the system was established, while we possess the power to restrain it from going outside those limits. From the necessities of the case, we should be compelled to form just such a government as our blessed fathers gave us ; and surely if they have so made it, that adds another reason why we should let slavery alone where it exists.

If I saw a venomous snake crawling in the road, any man would say I might seize the nearest stick and kill it ; but if I found that snake in bed with my children, that would be another question. I might hurt the children more than the snake, and it might bite them. Much more, if I found it in bed with my neighbour's children, and I had bound myself by a solemn compact not to meddle with his children under any circumstances, it would become me to let that particular mode of getting rid of the gentleman alone. But if there was a bed newly made up, to which the children were to be taken, and it was proposed to take a batch of young snakes and put them there with them, I take it no man would say there was any question how I ought to decide !

"That is just the case. The new Territories are the newly made bed to which our children are to go, and it lies with the nation to say whether they shall have snakes mixed up with them or not. It does not seem as if there could be much hesitation what our policy should be. . . ."

[After adverting to several of the arguments of the proslavery Democrats, as 'bushwhacking,' he continued : —]

". . . Another is John Brown ! You stir up insurrections ; you invade the South ! John Brown ! Harper's Ferry ! Why, John Brown was not a Republican ! You have never implicated a single Republican in that Harper's Ferry enterprise. We tell you if any member of the Republican party is guilty in that matter, you know it or you do not know it. If you do know it, you are inexcusable not to designate the man and prove the fact. If you do not know it, you are inexcusable to assert it, and especially to persist in the assertion after you have tried and failed to make the proof. You need not be told that persisting in a charge which one does not know to be true, is simply a malicious slander. Some of you admit that no Republican designedly aided or encouraged the Harper's Ferry affair, but still insist that our doctrines and declarations necessarily lead to such results. We do not believe it. We know we hold to no doctrines and make no declarations which were not held to and made by our fathers who framed the government under which we live, and we cannot see how declarations that were patriotic when they made them are villainous when we make them. You never dealt fairly by us in relation to that affair, and I will say frankly that I know of nothing in your character that should lead us to suppose that you would. You had just been soundly thrashed in the elections in several States, and others were soon to come. You rejoiced at the occasion, and only were troubled that there were not three times as many killed in the affair. You were in evident glee; there was no sorrow for the killed, nor for the peace of Virginia disturbed. You were rejoicing that by charging Republicans with this thing, you might get an advantage of us in New York and the other States. You pulled that string as tightly as you could, but your very generous and worthy expectations were not quite fulfilled. Each Republican knew that the charge was a slander, as to himself at least, and was not inclined by it to cast his vote in your favour. It was mere bushwhacking because you had nothing else to do. You are still on that track, and I say go on! If you think you can slander a woman into loving you or a man into voting for you, try it until you are satisfied.

"Another specimen of this bushwhacking, — that 'shoe strike.' Now, be it understood that I do not pretend to know all about the matter. I am merely going to speculate a little about some of its phases; and, at the outset, I am glad to see that a system of labour prevails in New England under which labourers can strike when they want to; when they are not obliged to work under all circumstances, and are not tied down and obliged to labour whether you pay them or not! I like the system which lets a man quit when he wants to, and wish it might prevail everywhere. One of the reasons why I am opposed to slavery is just here. What is the true condition of the labourer? I take it that it is best for all to leave each man free to acquire property as fast as he can. Some will get wealthy. I don't believe in a law to prevent a man from getting rich; it would do more harm than good. So while we do not propose any war upon capital, we do wish to allow the humblest man an equal chance to get rich with everybody else. When one starts poor, as most do in the race of life free society is such that when he knows he can better his condition, he knows that there is no fixed condition of labour for his whole life. I am not ashamed to confess that twenty-five years ago I was a hired labourer, mauling rails, at work on a flat-boat — just what might happen to any poor man's son. I want every man to have the chance — and I believe a black man is entitled to it — in which he can better his condition ; when he may look forward and hope to be a hired labourer this year, and the next work for himself afterward, and finally to hire men to work for him. That is the true system. Up here in New England you have a soil that scarcely sprouts black-eyed beans, and yet where will you find wealthy men so wealthy, and poverty so rarely in extremity? There is not another such place on earth ! I desire that if you get too thick here, and find it hard to better your condition on this soil, you may have a chance to strike and go somewhere else, where you may not be degraded, nor have your family corrupted by forced rivalry with negro slaves. I want you to have a clean bed and no snakes in it. Then you can better your condition, and so it may go on and on in one ceaseless round so long as man exists on the face of the earth.

" Now to come back to this shoe strike. If,

as the senator from Illinois asserts, this is caused by the withdrawal of Southern votes, consider briefly how you will meet the difficulty. You have done nothing, and have protested that you have done nothing, to injure the South; and yet to get back the shoe trade you must leave off doing something that you are now doing. What is it? You must stop thinking slavery wrong. Let your institutions be wholly changed; let your State constitutions be subverted; glorify slavery; and so you will get back the shoe trade — for what? You have brought owned labour with it to compete with your own labour, to underwork you and to degrade you. Are you ready to get back the trade on those terms?

" But the statement is not correct. You have not lost that trade; orders were never better than now. Senator Mason, a Democrat, comes into the Senate in homespun: a proof that the dissolution of the Union has actually begun. But orders are the same. Your factories have not struck work, neither those where they make anything for coats, nor for pants, nor for shirts, nor for ladies' dresses. Mr. Mason has not reached the manufacturers who ought to have made him a coat and pants. To make his proof good for anything, he should have come into the Senate barefoot.

"Another bushwhacking contrivance, — simply that, nothing else! I find a good many people who are very much concerned about the loss of Southern trade. Now, either these people are sincere or they are not. I will speculate a little about that. If they are sincere, and are moved by any real danger of the loss of Southern trade, they will simply get their names on the white list, and then instead of persuading Republicans to do likewise, they will be glad to keep you away. Don't you see they are thus shutting off competition? They would not be whispering around to Republicans to come in and share the profits with them. But if they are not sincere, and are merely trying to fool Republicans out of their votes, they will grow very anxious about your pecuniary prospects; they are afraid you are going to get broken up and ruined; they did not care about Democratic votes — oh no, no, no! You must judge which class those belong to whom you meet. I leave it to you to determine from the facts."

His Letter to Hon. Geo. Ashmun, President, accepting his Nomination for the Presidency.

May 23, 1860.

I accept the nomination tendered me by the Convention over which you presided, and of which I am formally apprised in the letter of yourself and others, acting as a committee of the Convention for that purpose.

The declaration of principles and sentiments which accompanies your letter, meets my approval; and it shall be my care not to violate or disregard it in any part.

Imploring the assistance of Divine Providence, and with due regard to the views and feelings of all who were represented in the Convention; to the rights of all the States and Territories and people of the nation; to the inviolability of the Constitution; and the perpetual union, harmony, and prosperity of all, — I am most happy to co-operate for the practical success of the principles declared by the Convention.

Your obliged friend and fellow-citizen,

A. Lincoln.

To the Citizens of Springfield, on his Departure for Washington.

February 11, 1861.

My Friends: No one, not in my position, can appreciate the sadness I feel at this parting. To this people I owe all that I am. Here I have lived more than a quarter of a century; here my children were born, and here one of them lies buried. I know not how soon I shall see you again. A duty devolves upon me which is, perhaps, greater than that which has devolved upon any other man since the days of Washington. He never would have succeeded except by the aid of Divine Providence, upon which he at all times relied. I feel that I cannot succeed without the same Divine aid which sustained him, and on the same Almighty Being I place my reliance for support; and I hope you, my friends, will all pray that I may receive that Divine assistance, without which I cannot succeed, but with which success is certain. Again I bid you an affectionate farewell.

FROM HIS REMARKS AT INDIANAPOLIS, INDIANA.

February 11, 1861.

"When the people rise in mass in behalf of the Union and the liberties of their country, truly may it be said ' The gates of hell cannot prevail against them.' In all trying positions in which I shall be placed, — and doubtless I shall be placed in many such, — my reliance will be placed upon you and the people of the United States; and I wish you to remember, now and forever, that it is your business and not mine; that if the Union of these States and the liberties of this people shall be lost, it is but little to any one man of fifty-two years of age, but a great deal to the thirty millions of people who inhabit these United States, and to their posterity in all coming time. It is your business to rise up and preserve the Union and liberty for yourselves, and not for me.

"I desire that [all duties] should be constitutionally performed. I, as already intimated, am but an accidental instrument, temporary, and to serve but for a limited time; and I appeal to you again, to constantly bear in mind, that with you, and not with politicians, not with presidents, not with office-seekers, but with you is the question, Shall the Union, and shall the liberties of this country, be preserved to the latest generation?"

From his Address to the Legislature at
Indianapolis, Indiana.

February 12, 1861.

" . . . Solomon says 'there is a time to keep
silence,' and when men wrangle by the mouth
with no certainty that they mean the same thing
while using the same word, it perhaps were as well
if they would keep silence.

"The words 'coercion' and 'invasion' are
much used in these days, and often with some
temper and hot blood. Let us make sure, if we
can, that we do not misunderstand the meaning
of those who use them. Let us get exact defini-
tions of these words, not from dictionaries, but
from the men themselves, who certainly deprecate
the things they would represent by the use of
words. What then is *coercion?* what is *invasion?*
Would the marching of an army into South Carolina, without the consent of her people and with
hostile intent towards them, be invasion? I certainly think it would; and it would be coercion
also, if the South Carolinians were forced to submit. But if the United States should merely re-
take and hold its own forts and other property, and
collect the duties on foreign importations, or even
withhold the mails from places where they were

15

habitually violated, would any or all these things be invasion or coercion? Do our professed lovers of the Union, but who spitefully resolve that they will resist coercion and invasion, understand that such things as these, on the part of the United States, would be coercion or invasion of a State? If so, their idea of means to preserve the object of their affection would seem exceedingly thin and airy. If sick, the little pills of the homœopathist would be much too large for them to swallow. In their view, the Union as a family relation would seem to be no regular marriage, but a sort of free-love arrangement to be maintained only on *passional attraction.* . . .

"In what consists the special sacredness of a State? I speak not of the position assigned to a State in the Union by the Constitution; for that, by the bond, we all recognise. That position, however, a State cannot carry out of the Union with it. I speak of that assumed primary right of a State to rule all which is *less* than itself, and ruin all which is larger than itself. If a State and a county in a given case should be equal in extent of territory, and equal in number of inhabitants, in what, as a matter of principle, is the State better than the county? Would an exchange of *names* be an exchange of *rights* upon principle? On what rightful principle may a State, being not more than one-fiftieth part of the nation in soil and population, break up the nation, and then coerce a proportionally larger subdivision of itself in the most arbitrary way? What mysterious right to play tyrant is conferred on a district of country, with its people, by merely calling it a State?

" Fellow-citizens, I am not asserting anything : I am merely asking questions for you to consider.

FROM HIS ADDRESS TO THE LEGISLATURE AT CO-
LUMBUS, OHIO.

February 13, 1861.

" It is true, as has been said by the president of the Senate, that a very great responsibility rests upon me in the position to which the votes of the American people have called me. I am deeply sensible of that weighty responsibility. I cannot but know, what you all know, that without a name, perhaps without a reason why I should have a name, there has fallen upon me a task such as did not rest even upon the Father of his Country ; and so feeling, I cannot but turn and look for that support without which it will be impossible for me to perform that great task. I turn then, and look to the great American people, and to that God who has never forsaken them. Allusion has been made to the interest felt in relation to the policy of the new Administration. In this I have received from some a degree of credit for having kept silence, and from others, some deprecation. I still think I was right.

" In the varying and repeatedly shifting scenes of the present, and without a precedent which could enable me to judge by the past, it has seemed fitting that before speaking upon the difficulties of the country, I should have gained a view of the whole field, being at liberty to modify and change the course of policy as future events may make a change necessary.

" I have not maintained silence from any want of real anxiety. It is a good thing that there is no more than anxiety, for there is nothing going wrong. It is a consoling circumstance that when we look out, there is nothing that really hurts anybody. We entertain different views upon political questions, but nobody is suffering anything. This is a most consoling circumstance, and from it we may conclude that all we want is time, patience, and a reliance on that God who has never forsaken this people."

FROM HIS REMARKS AT PITTSBURGH, PENNSYLVANIA.

February 15, 1861.

". . . The condition of the country is an extraordinary one, and fills the mind of every patriot with anxiety. It is my intention to give this subject all the consideration I possibly can, before specially deciding in regard to it, so that when I do speak, it may be as nearly right as possible. When I do speak, I hope I may say nothing in opposition to the spirit of the Constitution, contrary to the integrity of the Union, or which will prove inimical to the liberties of the people or to the peace of the whole country. And furthermore, when the time arrives for me to speak on this great subject, I hope I may say nothing to disappoint the people generally throughout the country, especially if the expectation has been based upon anything which I have heretofore said.

". . . If the great American people only keep their temper on both sides of the line, the troubles will come to an end, and the question which now distracts the country will be settled, just as surely as all other difficulties of a like character which have originated in this government have been adjusted. Let the people on both sides keep

their self-possession, and just as other clouds
have cleared away in due time, so will this great
nation continue to prosper as heretofore.

" . . . It is often said that the tariff is the
specialty of Pennsylvania. Assuming that direct
taxation is not to be adopted, the tariff question
must be as durable as the government itself. It
is a question of national housekeeping. It is to
the government what replenishing the meal-tub
is to the family. Ever varying circumstances will
require frequent modifications as to the amount
needed and the sources of supply. So far there
is little difference of opinion among the people.
It is only whether, and how far, duties on imports
shall be adjusted to favor home productions. In
the home market that controversy begins. One
party insists that too much protection oppresses
one class for the advantage of another; while
the other party argues that, with all its incidents,
in the long run all classes are benefited. In the
Chicago platform there is a plank upon this subject, which should be a general law to the incoming Administration. We should do neither more
nor less than we gave the people reason to believe
we would when they gave us their votes. . . .

" ' That while providing revenue for the support
of the general government by duties upon imports,

sound policy requires such an adjustment of these imposts as will encourage the development of the industrial interest of the whole country ; and we commend that policy of national exchanges which secures to working-men liberal wages, to agriculture remunerating prices, to mechanics and manufacturers adequate reward for their skill, labour, and enterprise, and to the nation commercial prosperity and independence.'

" . . . My political education strongly inclines me against a very free use of any of the means by the Executive to control the legislation of the country. As a rule, I think it better that Congress should originate as well as perfect its measures without external bias. I therefore would rather recommend to every gentleman who knows he is to be a member of the next Congress, to take an enlarged view, and post himself thoroughly, so as to contribute his part to such an adjustment of the tariff as shall provide a sufficient revenue, and in its other bearings, so far as possible, be just and equal to all sections of the country and classes of the people."

FROM HIS ADDRESS AT TRENTON, TO THE SENATE
OF NEW JERSEY.

February 21, 1861.

" . . . May I be pardoned if, upon this occasion, I mention that away back in my childhood, the earliest days of my being able to read, I got hold of a small book, such a one as few of the younger members have ever seen, — 'Weems's Life of Washington.' I remember all the accounts there given of the battlefields and struggles for the liberties of the country, and none fixed themselves upon my imagination so deeply as the struggle here at Trenton, New Jersey. The crossing of the river, the contest with the Hessians, the great hardships endured at that time, — all fixed themselves upon my memory more than any single Revolutionary event; and you all know, for you have all been boys, how those early impressions last longer than any others. I recollect thinking then, boy even though I was, that there must have been something more than common that these men struggled for. I am exceedingly anxious that that thing — that something even more than national independence; that something that held out a great promise to all the people of the world for all time to come

— I am exceedingly anxious that this Union, this Constitution, and the liberties of the people shall be perpetuated in accordance with the original idea for which that struggle was made ; and I shall be most happy indeed, if I shall be a humble instrument in the hands of the Almighty, and of this his almost chosen people, for perpetuating the object of that great struggle. You give me this reception, as I understand, without distinction of party. I learn that this body is composed of a majority of gentlemen, who, in the exercise of their best judgment in the choice of a chief magistrate, did not think I was the man. I understand, nevertheless, that they came forward here to greet me as the constitutionally elected President of the United States, — as citizens of the United States to meet the man who, for the time being, is the representative of the majesty of the nation, — united by the single purpose to perpetuate the Constitution, the Union, and the liberties of the people. As such I accept this reception more gratefully than I could do, did I believe it was tendered to me as an individual."

ADDRESS AT INDEPENDENCE HALL, PHILADELPHIA.

February 22, 1861.

" I AM filled with deep emotion at finding myself standing in this place, where were collected together the wisdom, the patriotism, the devotion to principle, from which sprang the institutions under which we live. You have kindly suggested to me that in my hands is the task of restoring peace to our distracted country. I can say in return, Sir, that all the political sentiments I entertain have been drawn, so far as I have been able to draw them, from the sentiments which originated in and were given to the world from this hall. I have never had a feeling, politically, that did not spring from the sentiments embodied in the Declaration of Independence. I have often pondered over the dangers which were incurred by the men who assembled here, and framed and adopted that Declaration of Independence. I have pondered over the toils that were endured by the officers and soldiers of the army who achieved that independence. I have often inquired of myself what great principle or idea it was that kept this Confederacy so long together. It was not the mere matter of the separation of the colonies from the motherland, but that sentiment in the Declaration of Independence which gave liberty, not alone to the people of this country, but hope to all the world for all future time. It was that which gave promise that in due time the weight would be lifted from the shoulders of all men, and that all should have an equal chance. This is the sentiment embodied in the Declaration of Independence. Now, my friends, can this country be saved on that basis? If it can, I will consider myself one of the happiest men in the world if I can help to save it. If it cannot be saved upon that principle, it will be truly awful. But if this country cannot be saved without giving up that principle, I was about to say I would rather be assassinated on this spot than surrender it. Now, in my view of the present aspect of affairs, there need be no bloodshed or war. There is no necessity for it. I am not in favour of such a course ; and I may say in advance that there will be no bloodshed unless it is forced upon the Government, and then it will be compelled to act in self-defence. The government will not use force, unless force is used against it. . . ."

From his Reply to the Governor, and his
Address to the Legislature at Harris-
burgh, Pennsylvania.

February 22, 1861.

". . . I thank you most sincerely for this reception, and the generous words in which support
has been promised me upon this occasion. I
thank your great Commonwealth for the overwhelming support it recently gave, not me personally, but the cause which I think a just one, in the
late election.

Allusion has been made to the fact — the interesting fact, perhaps we should say — that I for the
first time appear at the capital of the great Commonwealth of Pennsylvania upon the birthday of
the Father of his Country.   In connection with
that beloved anniversary connected with the history of this country, I have already gone through
one exceedingly interesting scene this morning
in the ceremonies at Philadelphia.   Under the
kind conduct of gentlemen there, I was for the
first time allowed the privilege of standing in old
Independence Hall to have a few words addressed
to me there, and opening up to me an opportunity of manifesting, with much regret, that I
had not more time to express something of my

own feelings excited by the occasion, that had been really the feelings of my whole life.

Besides this, our friends there had provided a magnificent flag of the country. They had arranged it so that I was given the honour of raising it to the head of its staff. And when it went up, I was pleased that it went to its place by the strength of my own feeble arm, when, according to the arrangement, the cord was pulled, and it floated gloriously to the wind without an accident, in the light, glowing sunshine of the morning. I could not help hoping that there was in the entire success of that beautiful ceremony at least something of an omen of what is to come. How could I help feeling there as I often have felt? In the whole of that proceeding, I was a very humble instrument. I had not provided the flag; I had not made the arrangement for elevating it to its place; I had applied but a very small portion of my feeble strength in raising it. In the whole transaction, I was in the hands of the people who had arranged it; and if I can have the same generous co-operation of the people of the nation, I think the flag of our country may yet be kept flaunting gloriously.

I recur for a moment but to repeat some words uttered at the hotel, in regard to what has been said about the military support which the General Government may expect from the Commonwealth of Pennsylvania in a proper emergency. To guard against any possible mistake do I recur to this. It is not with any pleasure that I contemplate the possibility that a necessity may arise in this country for the use of the military arm. While I am exceedingly gratified to see the manifestation upon your streets of your military force here, and exceedingly gratified at your promises here to use that force upon a proper emergency — while I make these acknowledgments, I desire to repeat, in order to preclude any possible misconstruction, that I do most sincerely hope that we shall have no use for them ; that it will never become their duty to shed blood, and most especially never to shed fraternal blood. I promise that, so far as I may have wisdom to direct, if so painful a result shall in any wise be brought about, it shall be through no fault of mine. . . ."

REPLY TO THE MAYOR OF WASHINGTON, D. C.

February 27, 1861.

" MR. MAYOR : I thank you, and through you the municipal authorities of this city who accompany you, for this welcome. And as it is the first time in my life, since the present phase of politics has presented itself in this country, that I have said anything publicly within a region of country where the institution of slavery exists, I will take this occasion to say that I think very much of the ill-feeling that has existed and still exists between the people in the section from which I came and the people here, is dependent upon a misunderstanding of one another. I therefore avail myself of this opportunity to assure you, Mr. Mayor, and all the gentlemen present, that I have not now, and never have had, any other than as kindly feelings towards you as to the people of my own section. I have not now and never have had any disposition to treat you in any respect otherwise than as my own neighbours. I have not now any purpose to withhold from you any of the benefits of the Constitution under any circumstances, that I would not feel myself constrained to withhold from my own neighbours ; and I hope, in a word, that when we become better acquainted, — and I say it with great confidence, — we shall like each other the more. . . . "

From the First Inaugural Address.

March 4, 1861.

" . . . Apprehension seems to exist among the people of the Southern States, that by the accession of a Republican Administration their property and their peace and personal security are to be endangered. There has never been any reasonable cause for such apprehension. Indeed, the most ample evidence to the contrary has all the while existed and been open to their inspection. It is found in nearly all the published speeches of him who now addresses you. I do but quote from one of those speeches when I declare that 'I have no purpose, directly or indirectly, to interfere with the institution of slavery in the States where it exists. I believe I have no lawful right to do so, and I have no inclination to do so.' . . . I only press upon the public attention the most conclusive evidence of which the case is susceptible, that the property, peace, and security of no section are to be in any wise endangered by the now incoming Administration. I add, too, that all the protection which, consistently with the Constitution and the laws, can be given, will cheerfully be given to all the States, when lawfully demanded for whatever cause, as cheerfully to one section as to another.

" . . . I take the official oath to-day with no mental reservations, and with no purpose to construe the Constitution or the laws by any hypercritical rules. And while I do not choose now to specify particular acts of Congress as proper to be enforced, I do suggest that it will be much safer for all, both in official and private stations, to conform to and abide by all those acts which stand unrepealed, than to violate any of them, trusting to find impunity in having them held to be unconstitutional.

" It is seventy-two years since the first inauguration of a President under our National Constitution. During that period fifteen different and greatly distinguished citizens have, in succession, administered the Executive branch of the government. They have conducted it through many perils, and generally with great success. Yet, with all this scope of precedent, I now enter upon the same great task for the brief constitutional term of four years, under great and peculiar difficulty. A disruption of the Federal Union, heretofore only menaced, is now formidably attempted.

" I hold that, in contemplation of universal law,

16

and of the Constitution, *the Union of these States is perpetual.* Perpetuity is implied, if not expressed, in the fundamental law of all National Governments. It is safe to assert that no government proper ever had a provision in its organic law for its own termination. Continue to execute all the express provisions of our National Government, and the Union will endure forever, — it being impossible to destroy it, except by some action not provided for in the instrument itself.

" Again, if the United States be not a government proper, but an association of States in the nature of contract merely, can it as a contract be peaceably unmade by less than all the parties who made it? One party to a contract may violate it — break it, so to speak ; but does it not require all to lawfully rescind it?

" . . . It follows then, from these views, that no State, upon its own mere motion, can lawfully get out of the Union ; that resolves and ordinances to that effect are legally void ; and acts of violence within any State or States, against the authority of the United States, are insurrectionary or revolutionary according to circumstances.

" I therefore consider that, in view of the Constitution and the laws, the Union is unbroken ;

and to the extent of my ability, I shall take care, as the Constitution itself expressly enjoins upon me, that the laws of the Union be faithfully executed in all the States. Doing this, I deem to be only a simple duty on my part; and I shall perform it, so far as practicable, unless my rightful masters, the American people, shall withhold the requisite means, or in some authoritative manner direct the contrary. I trust this will not be regarded as a menace, but only as the declared purpose of the Union, that it will constitutionally defend and maintain itself.

" In doing this there need be no bloodshed or violence; and there shall be none, unless it be forced upon the national authority. The power confided to me will be used to hold, occupy, and possess the property and places belonging to the government, and to collect the duties and imposts; but beyond what may be but necessary for these objects, there will be no invasion, no using of force against or among the people anywhere. . . .

" That there are persons in one section or another who seek to destroy the Union at all events, and are glad of any pretext to do it, I will neither affirm nor deny; but if there be such, I need address no word to them. To those, however, who really love the Union, may I not speak?

" Before entering upon so grave a matter as the destruction of our national fabric, with all its benefits, its memories, and its hopes, would it not be wise to ascertain precisely why we do it? Will you hazard so desperate a step while there is any possibility that any portion of the ills you fly from, have no real existence? Will you, while the certain ills you fly to are greater than all the real ones you fly from — will you risk the commission of so fearful a mistake?

" All profess to be content in the Union, if all constitutional rights can be maintained. Is it true, then, that any right plainly written in the Constitution has been denied? I think not. Happily the human mind is so constituted that no party can reach to the audacity of doing this. Think, if you can, of a single instance in which a plainly written provision of the Constitution has ever been denied? . . .

" I do not forget the position assumed by some, that constitutional questions are to be decided by the Supreme Court; nor do I deny that such decisions must be binding, in any case, upon the parties to the suit, as to the object of that suit, while they are also entitled to very high respect and consideration in all parallel cases by all other departments of the government. . . . At the same time, . . . if the policy of the government upon vital questions, affecting the whole people, is to be irrevocably fixed by decisions of the Supreme Court, . . . the people will have ceased to be their own rulers, having to that extent practically resigned their government into the hands of that eminent tribunal. . . .

" Nor is there in this view any assault upon the Court or the judges. . . . One section of our country believes slavery is right and ought to be extended, while the other believes it is wrong and ought not to be extended. This is the only substantial dispute. The fugitive-slave clause of the Constitution, and the law for the suppression of the foreign slave trade are each as well enforced, perhaps, as any law ever can be in a community where the moral sense of the people imperfectly supports the law itself. The great body of the people abide by the dry, legal obligation in both cases, and a few break over in each. This, I think, cannot be perfectly cured; and it would be worse, in both cases, after the separation of the sections than before. The foreign slave trade, now imperfectly suppressed, would be ultimately revived, without restriction, in one section, while fugitive slaves, now only partially surrendered, would not be surrendered at all by the other.

"Physically speaking, we cannot separate. We cannot remove our respective sections from each other nor build an impassable wall between them. A husband and wife may be divorced, and go out of the presence and beyond the reach of each other; but the different parts of our country cannot do this. They cannot but remain face to face; and intercourse, either amicable or hostile, must continue between them. Is it possible, then, to make that intercourse more advantageous or more satisfactory after separation than before? Can aliens make treaties easier than friends can make laws? Can treaties be more faithfully enforced between aliens than laws among friends? Suppose you go to war, you cannot fight always; and when, after much loss on both sides and no gain on either, you cease fighting, the identical old questions as to terms of intercourse are again upon you. . . .

"The Chief Magistrate derives all his authority from the people, and they have conferred none upon him to fix terms for the separation of the States. The people themselves can do this also, if they choose; but the Executive, as such, has nothing to do with it. His duty is to administer the present government as it came to his hands, and to transmit it, unimpaired by him, to his successor.

"Why should there not be a patient confidence in the ultimate justice of the people? Is there any better or equal hope in the world? In our present differences, is either party without faith of being in the right? If the Almighty Ruler of Nations with His eternal truth and justice be on your side of the North, or on yours of the South, that truth and that justice will surely prevail, by the judgment of this great tribunal of the American people.

". . . My countrymen, one and all, think calmly and well upon this whole subject. Nothing valuable can be lost by taking time. If there be an object to hurry any of you in hot haste to a step which you would never take deliberately, that object will be frustrated by taking time; but no good object can be frustrated by it. Such of you as are now dissatisfied, still have the old Constitution, unimpaired, and on the sensitive point the laws of your own framing under it; while the new Administration will have no immediate power, if it would, to change either. If it were admitted that you who are dissatisfied hold the right side in the dispute, there still is no single good reason for precipitate action. Intelligence, patriotism, Christianity, and a firm reliance on Him who has never yet forsaken this favoured land are still competent to adjust in the best way all our present difficulty.

" In your hands, my dissatisfied fellow-country-men, and not in mine, is the momentous issue of civil war. The government will not assail you. You can have no conflict without being your-selves the aggressors. You have no oath regis-tered in Heaven to destroy the government, while I shall have the most solemn one to 'pre-serve, protect, and defend it.'

" I am loath to close. We are not enemies, but friends. We must not be enemies. Though passion may have strained, it must not break our bonds of affection.

" The mystic chords of memory, stretching from every battlefield and patriot grave to every living heart and hearthstone all over this broad land, will yet swell the chorus of the Union when again touched, as surely they will be, by the better angels of our nature."

FROM HIS FIRST MESSAGE TO CONGRESS, AT THE
SPECIAL SESSION, JULY 4, 1861.

July 4, 1861.

" . . . It is thus seen that the assault upon and
reduction of Fort Sumter was in no sense a matter
of self-defence on the part of the assailants. They
well knew that the garrison in the fort could by
no possibility commit aggression upon them.
They knew — they were expressly notified — that
the giving of bread to the few brave and hungry
men of the garrison was all which would on that
occasion be attempted, unless themselves, by re-
sisting so much, should provoke more. They
knew that this government desired to keep the
garrison in the fort, not to assail them, but merely
to maintain visible possession, and thus to preserve the Union from actual and immediate dissolution, — trusting, as hereinbefore stated, to time,
discussion, and the ballot-box, for final adjustment ; and they assailed and reduced the fort
for precisely the reverse object, — to drive out
the visible authority of the Federal Union, and
thus force it to immediate dissolution.

" . . . By the affair at Fort Sumter, . . . the
assailants of the government began the conflict

of arms, without a gun in sight, or in expectancy
to return their fire, save only the few in the fort
sent to that harbour years before for their own
protection, and still ready to give that protection
in whatever was lawful. In this act, discarding
all else, they have forced upon the country the
distinct issue, ' immediate dissolution or blood.'

" And this issue embraces more than the fate
of these United States. It presents to the whole
family of man the question whether a constitutional republic or democracy — a government of
the people by the same people — can or cannot
maintain its territorial integrity against its own
domestic foes. It presents the question whether
discontented individuals, too few in numbers to
control administration according to organic law
in any case, can always, upon the pretences made
in this case or any other pretences, or arbitrarily
without any pretence, break up their government,
and thus practically put an end to free government upon the earth. It forces us to ask : ' Is
there, in all republics, this inherent and fatal
weakness?' 'Must a government, of necessity,
be too strong for the liberties of its own people,
or too weak to maintain its own existence?'

" So viewing the issue, no choice was left but to
call out the war power of the government, and

so to resist force employed for its destruction by force for its preservation.

" The call was made, and the response of the country was most gratifying, surpassing in unanimity and spirit the most sanguine expectation.

" . . . The people of Virginia have thus allowed this giant insurrection to make its nest within her borders, — and this government has no choice left but to deal with it where it finds it. And it has the less regret, as the loyal citizens have in due form claimed its protection. Those loyal citizens this government is bound to recognise and protect, as being Virginia.

" In the border States, so called, — in fact, the Middle States, — there are those who favour a policy which they call ' armed neutrality ; ' that is, an arming of those States to prevent the Union forces passing one way, or the disunion the other, over their soil. This would be disunion completed. Figuratively speaking, it would be the building of an impassable wall along the line of separation, — and yet not quite an impassable one, for under the guise of neutrality, it would tie the hands of Union men, and freely pass supplies from among them to the insurrectionists, which it could not do as an open enemy. At a stroke, it would take all the trouble off the hands of secession, except only what proceeds from the external blockade. It would do for the disunion-ists that which of all things they most desire, — feed them well and give them disunion without a struggle of their own. It recognises no fidelity to the Constitution, no obligation to maintain the Union ; and while very many who have favoured it are doubtless loyal citizens, it is, nevertheless, very injurious in effect.

" . . . The forbearance of this government had been so extraordinary and so long continued, as to lead some foreign nations to shape their action as if they supposed the early destruction of our National Union was probable. While this, on discovery, gave the Executive some concern, he is now happy to say that the sovereignty and rights of the United States are now every-where practically respected by foreign powers, and a general sympathy with the country is mani-fested throughout the world.

" . . . It might seem at first thought to be of little difference whether the present movement at the South be called *secession* or *rebellion*. The movers, however, well understand the difference. At the beginning they knew they could never raise their treason to any respectable magnitude by any name which implies violation of law. They knew their people possessed as much of moral sense, as much of devotion to law and order, and as much pride in and reverence for the history and government of their common country as any other civilised and patriotic people. They knew they could make no advancement directly in the teeth of these strong and noble sentiments. Accordingly, they commenced by an insidious debauching of the public mind. They invented an ingenious sophism which, if conceded, was followed by perfectly logical steps, through all the incidents, to the complete destruction of the Union. The sophism itself is that any State of the Union may consistently with the national Constitution, and therefore lawfully and peacefully, withdraw from the Union without the consent of the Union or of any other State. The little disguise that the supposed right is to be exercised only for just cause, themselves to be the sole judges of its justice, is too thin to merit any notice.

" With rebellion thus *sugar-coated* they have been drugging the public mind of their section for more than thirty years, and until at length they have brought many good men to a willingness to take up arms against the government the day after some assemblage of men have enacted the farcical pretence of taking their State out of the Union, who could have been brought to no such thing the day before.

"This sophism derives much, perhaps the whole of its currency from the assumption that there is some omnipotent and sacred supremacy pertaining to a State — to each State of our Federal Union. Our States have neither more nor less power than that reserved to them in the Union by the Constitution, no one of them ever having been a State out of the Union. The original ones passed into the Union even before they cast off their British colonial dependence, and the new ones each came into the Union directly from a condition of dependence, excepting Texas. And even Texas in its temporary independence was never designated a State. The new ones only took the designation of States on coming into the Union, while that name was first adopted for the old ones in and by the Declaration of Independence. Therein the 'United Colonies' were declared to be 'free and independent States;' but even then the object plainly was, not to declare their independence of one another or of the Union, but directly the contrary, as their mutual pledges and their mutual action before, at the time, and afterward abundantly show. The express plighting of faith by each and all of the original thirteen in the Articles of Confederation two years later, that the Union shall be perpetual, is most conclusive. Having never been States, either in substance or name, outside of the Union, whence this magical omnipotence of 'State-Rights,' asserting a claim of power to lawfully destroy the Union itself? Much is said about the 'sovereignty' of the States; but the word is not in the National Constitution, nor, as is believed, in any of the State constitutions. What is *sovereignty* in the political sense of the term? Would it be far wrong to define it 'a political community without a political superior?' Tested by this, no one of our States, except Texas, ever was a sovereignty. And even Texas gave up the character on coming into the Union, by which act she acknowledged the Constitution of the United States, and the laws and treaties of the United States made in pursuance of the Constitution, to be for her the supreme law of the land. The States have their status in the Union, and they have no other legal status. If they break from this, they can only do so against law and by revolution. The Union, and not themselves separately, procured their independence and their liberty. By conquest or purchase, the Union gave each of them what-

ever of independence or liberty it has. The
Union is older than any of the States, and, in
fact, it created them as States. Originally some
dependent colonies made the Union, and in turn
the Union threw off their old dependence for
them, and made them States, such as they are.
Not one of them ever had a State constitution
independent of the Union. Of course it is not
forgotten that all the new States framed their
constitutions before they entered the Union, —
nevertheless, dependent upon and preparatory
to coming into the Union.

" . . . It may be affirmed without extravagance
that the free institutions we enjoy have developed
the powers and improved the condition of our
whole people, beyond any example in the world.
Of this we now have a striking and an impres-
sive illustration. So large an army as the government has now on foot was never before known,
without a soldier in it but who has taken his place
there of his own free choice. But more than this,
there are many single regiments, whose members,
one and another, possess full practical knowledge
of all the arts, sciences, and professions, and whatever else, whether useful or elegant, is known in
the world ; and there is scarcely one from which
there could not be selected a President, a cabinet,

a congress, and perhaps a court, abundantly competent to administer the government itself. Nor do I say that this is not true also in the army of our late friends, now adversaries in this contest; but if it is, so much the better reason why the government which has conferred such benefits on both them and us should not be broken up. Whoever in any section proposes to abandon such a government, would do well to consider in deference to what principle it is that he does it; what better he is likely to get in its stead; whether the substitute will give, or be intended to give, so much of good to the people? There are some foreshadowings on this subject. Our adversaries have adopted some declarations of independence in which, unlike the good old one penned by Jefferson, they omit the words, 'all men are created equal.' Why? They have adopted a temporary national constitution, in the preamble of which, unlike our good old one signed by Washington, they omit 'We, the people,' and substitute 'We, the deputies of the sovereign and independent States.' Why? Why this deliberate pressing out of view the rights of men and the authority of the people?

"This is essentially a people's contest. On the side of the Union it is a struggle for maintaining in the world that form and substance of government whose leading object is to elevate the condition of men, — to lift artificial weights from all shoulders, to clear the paths of laudable pursuit for all, to afford all an unfettered start and a fair chance in the race of life. Yielding to partial and temporary departures from necessity, this is the leading object of the government for the existence of which we contend.

"... Our popular government has often been called an experiment. Two points in it our people have already settled, — the successful establishing and the successful administering of it. One still remains, — its successful maintainance against a formidable internal attempt to overthrow it. It is now for them to demonstrate to the world that those who can fairly carry an election can also suppress a rebellion ; that ballots are the rightful and peaceful successors of bullets ; and that when ballots have fairly and constitutionally decided, there can be no successful appeal back to bullets ; that there can be no successful appeal, except to ballots themselves, at succeeding elections. Such will be a great lesson of peace ; teaching men that what they cannot take by an election, neither can they take by a war ; teaching all the folly of being the beginners of a war."

December 3, 1861.

" . . . You will not be surprised to learn that
in the peculiar exigencies of the times, our intercourse with foreign nations has been attended
with profound solicitude, chiefly turning upon our
own domestic affairs.

"A disloyal portion of the American people
have, during the whole year, been engaged in an
attempt to divide and destroy the Union. A
nation which endures factious domestic division
is exposed to disrespect abroad ; and one party,
if not both, is sure, sooner or later, to invoke
foreign intervention. Nations thus tempted to
interfere are not always able to resist the
counsels of seeming expediency and ungenerous
ambition, although measures adopted under such
influences seldom fail to be injurious and unfortunate to those adopting them.

"The disloyal citizens of the United States
who have offered the ruin of our country in return
for the aid and comfort which they have invoked
abroad, have received less patronage and encouragement than they probably expected. If it were

just to suppose, as the insurgents have seemed to assume, that foreign nations in this case, discarding all moral, social, and treaty obligations, would act solely and selfishly for the most speedy restoration of commerce, including especially the acquisition of cotton, those nations appear as yet not to have seen their way to their object more directly or clearly through the destruction than through the preservation of the Union. . . .

" The principal lever relied on by the insurgents for exciting foreign nations to hostility against us, as already intimated, is the embarrassment of commerce. Those nations, however, not improbably saw from the first that it was the Union which made as well our foreign as our domestic commerce. They can scarcely have failed to perceive that the effort for disunion produces the existing difficulty; and that one strong nation promises a more durable peace and a more extensive, valuable, and reliable commerce than can the same nation broken into hostile fragments.

" . . . The operations of the treasury during the period which has elapsed since your adjournment have been conducted with signal success. The patriotism of the people has placed at the disposal of the government the large means demanded by the public exigencies. Much of the national loan has been taken by citizens of the industrial classes, whose confidence in their country's faith, and zeal for their country's deliverance from present peril have induced them to contribute to the support of the government the whole of their limited acquisitions. This fact imposes peculiar obligations to economy in disbursement and energy in action.

". . . The war continues. In considering the policy to be adopted for suppressing the insurrection, I have been anxious and careful that the inevitable conflict for this purpose should not degenerate into a violent and remorseless revolutionary struggle.

". . . The last ray of hope for preserving the Union peaceably, expired at the assault on Fort Sumter. . . . What was painfully uncertain then is much better defined and more distinct now; and the progress of events is plainly in the right direction.

". . . It continues to develop that the insurrection is largely, if not exclusively, a war upon the first principle of popular government, — the rights of the people. Conclusive evidence of this is found in the most grave and maturely considered public documents, as well as in the general tone of the insurgents. In those documents we find the abridgment of the existing right of suffrage, and the denial to the people of all right to participate in the selection of public officers, except the legislative, boldly advocated, with laboured arguments to prove that large control of the people in government is the source of all political evil. Monarchy itself is sometimes hinted at, as a possible refuge from the power of the people.

" In my present position, I could scarcely be justified were I to omit raising a warning voice against this approach of returning despotism.

" It is not needed nor fitting here that a general argument should be made in favour of popular institutions ; but there is one point, with its connections, not so hackneyed as most others, to which I ask a brief attention. It is the effort to place capital on an equal footing with, if not above, labour, in the structure of government. It is assumed that labour is available only in connection with capital ; that nobody labours, unless somebody else, owning capital, somehow, by the use of it, induces him to labour. This assumed, it is next considered whether it is best that capital shall hire labourers, and thus induce them to work by their own consent, or buy them and drive them to it without their consent. Having proceeded thus far, it is naturally concluded that all labourers are either hired labourers, or what we call slaves. And further, it is assumed that whoever is once a hired labourer is fixed in that condition for life.

" Now, there is no such relation between capital and labour as assumed, nor is there any such thing as a free man being fixed for life in the condition of a hired labourer. Both these assumptions are false, and all inferences from them are groundless.

" Labour is prior to and independent of capital. Capital is only the fruit of labour, and could never have existed if labour had not first existed. Labour is the superior of capital, and deserves much the higher consideration. Capital has its rights, which are as worthy of protection as any other rights. Nor is it denied that there is, and probably always will be, a relation between labour and capital, producing mutual benefits. The error is in assuming that the whole labour of the community exists within that relation. A few men own capital, and that few avoid labour themselves, and with their capital hire or buy another few to labour for them. A large majority belong to neither class, — neither work for others, nor have others working for them. In most of the Southern States, a majority of the whole people, of all colours, are neither slaves nor masters; while in the Northern, a majority are neither hirers nor hired.   Men with their families — wives, sons, and daughters — work for themselves, on their farms, in their houses, and in their shops, taking the whole product to themselves, and asking no favours of capital on the one hand, nor of hired labourers or slaves on the other.   It is not forgotten that a considerable number of persons mingle their own labour with capital, — that is, they labour with their own hands, and also buy or hire others to labour for them ; but this is only a mixed and not a distinct class.   No principle stated is disturbed by the existence of this mixed class.

"Again, as has already been said, there is not of necessity any such thing as the free, hired labourer being fixed to that condition for life. Many independent men, everywhere in these States, a few years back in their lives were hired labourers.   The prudent, penniless beginner in the world labours for wages awhile, saves a surplus with which to buy tools or land for himself, then labours on his own account another while, and at length hires another new beginner to help him. This is the just and generous and prosperous system which opens the way to all, gives hope to all, and consequent energy and progress and improvement of condition to all.   No men living are

more worthy to be trusted than those who toil
up from poverty, none less inclined to take or
touch aught which they have not honestly earned.
Let them beware of surrendering a political power
which they already possess, and which, if surrendered, will surely be used to close the door of
advancement against such as they, and to fix new
disabilities and burdens upon them, till all of
liberty shall be lost."

His Reply to the Lutheran Ministers.

May, 1862.

I welcome here the representatives of the
Evangelical Lutherans of the United States. I
accept with gratitude their assurances of the sympathy and support of that enlightened, influential,
and loyal class of my fellow-citizens, in an important crisis which involves, in my judgment, not
only the civil and religious liberties of mankind in
many countries and through many ages. You
well know, gentlemen, and the world knows, how
reluctantly I accepted this issue of battle, forced
upon me, on my advent to this place, by the internal enemies of our country. You all know —
the world knows — the forces and the resources
the public agents have brought into employment

to sustain a government against which there has been brought not one complaint of real injury committed against society at home or abroad.   You all may recollect that in taking up the sword thus forced into our hands, this government appealed to the prayers of the pious and the good, and declared that it placed its whole dependence upon the favour of God.   I now humbly and reverently, in your presence, reiterate the acknowledgment of that dependence, not doubting that, if it shall please the Divine Being who determines the destinies of nations, this shall remain a united people ; and that they will, humbly seeking the Divine guidance, make their prolonged national existence a source of new benefits to themselves and their successors, and to all classes and conditions of mankind.

FROM A LETTER TO GENERAL McCLELLAN.

May 9, 1862.

" . . . I have just assisted the Secretary of War in framing part of a despatch to you, relating to army corps, which despatch of course will have reached you long before this will.

" I wish to say a few words to you privately on this subject.   I ordered the army corps organisation, not only on the unanimous opinion of the twelve generals whom you had selected and assigned as generals of division, but also on the unanimous opinion of every *military man* I could get an opinion from (and every modern military book), yourself only excepted. Of course I did not on my own judgment pretend to understand the subject. I now think it indispensable for you to know how your struggle against it is received in quarters which we cannot entirely disregard. It is looked upon as merely an effort to pamper one or two pets and to persecute and degrade their supposed rivals. I have had no word from Sumner, Heintzelman, or Keyes. The commanders of these corps are of course the three highest officers with you, but I am constantly told that you have no consultation or communication with them, — that you consult and communicate with nobody but General Fitz John Porter, and perhaps General Franklin. I do not say these complaints are true or just, but at all events it is proper you should know of their existence. Do the commanders of corps disobey your orders in anything?

" . . . Are you strong enough — are you strong enough, even with my help — to set your foot upon the necks of Sumner, Heintzelman, and Keyes, all at once? This is a practical and a very serious question for you."

FROM HIS PROCLAMATION REVOKING GENERAL
    HUNTER'S ORDER SETTING THE SLAVES FREE;
    AND OFFERING COMPENSATED EMANCIPATION TO
    SLAVE OWNERS.

May 19, 1862.

"The resolution . . . was adopted by large
majorities in both branches of Congress, and now
stands an authentic, definite, and solemn proposal
of the nation to the States and people most immediately interested in the subject-matter. To
the people of those States I now earnestly appeal.
I do not argue — I beseech you to make arguments for yourselves. You cannot, if you would,
be blind to the signs of the times. I beg of you
a calm and enlarged consideration of them, rang-
ing, if it may be, far above personal and partisan
politics. The proposal makes common cause for
a common object, casting no reproaches upon any.
It acts not the Pharisee. The change it contemplates would come gently as the dews of heaven,
not rending or wrecking anything. Will you not
embrace it? So much good has not been done
by one effort in all past time as in the providence of God it is now your high privilege to do.
May the vast future not have to lament that you
have neglected it."

APPEAL TO THE BORDER STATES TO ACCEPT COMPENSATED EMANCIPATION.

July 12, 1862.

AFTER the adjournment of Congress, now near, I shall have no opportunity of seeing you for several months. Believing that you of the border States hold more power for good than any other equal number of members, I feel it a duty which I cannot justifiably waive, to make this appeal to you.

I intend no reproach or complaint when I assure you that, in my opinion, if you all had voted for the resolution in the gradual-emancipation message of last March, the war would now be substantially ended. And the plan therein proposed is yet one of the most potent and swift means of ending it. Let the States which are in rebellion see, definitely and certainly, that in no event will the States you represent ever join their proposed confederacy, and they cannot much longer maintain the contest. But you cannot divest them of their hope to ultimately have you with them, so long as you show a determination to perpetuate the institution within your own States. Beat them at elections, as you have overwhelmingly done, and, nothing daunted, they still claim you as their own. You and I know what the lever of their power is. Break that lever before their faces, and they can shake you no more forever.

Most of you have treated me with kindness and consideration, and I trust you will not now think I improperly touch what is exclusively your own, when, for the sake of the whole country I ask, Can you, for your States, do better than to take the course I urge? Discarding punctilio and maxims adapted to more manageable times, and looking only to the unprecedentedly stern facts of our case, can you do better in any possible event? You prefer that the constitutional relation of the States to the nation shall be practically restored without disturbance of the institution; and if this were done, my whole duty in this respect, under the Constitution and my oath of office, would be performed. But it is not done, and we are trying to accomplish it by war. The incidents of the war cannot be avoided. If the war continues long, as it must if the object be not sooner attained, the institution in your States will be extinguished by mere friction and abrasion, — by the mere incidents of the war. It will be gone, and you will have nothing valuable in lieu of it. Much of its value is gone already. How much better for you and for your people to take the step which at once shortens the war and secures substantial compensation for that which is sure to be wholly lost in any other event? How much better to thus save the money which else we sink forever in the war! How much better to do it while we can, lest the war ere long render us pecuniarily unable to do it! How much better for you as seller, and the nation as buyer, to sell out and buy out that without which the war could never have been, than to sink both the thing to be sold and the price of it in cutting one another's throats!

I do not speak of emancipation at once, but of a decision at once to emancipate gradually. Room in South America for colonisation can be obtained cheaply and in abundance, and when numbers shall be large enough to be company and encouragement for one another, the freed people will not be so reluctant to go.

I am pressed with a difficulty not yet mentioned, — one which threatens division among those who, united, are none too strong. General Hunter is an honest man. He was, and I hope still is, my friend. I valued him none the less for his agreeing with me in the general wish that all men everywhere could be free. He proclaimed all

men free within certain States, and I repudiated
the proclamation.   He expected more good and
less harm from the measure than I could believe
would follow.   Yet in repudiating it, I gave dis-
satisfaction if not offence to many whose support
the country cannot afford to lose.   And this is
not the end of it.   The pressure in this direction
is still upon me, and is increasing.   By conceding
what I now ask, you can relieve me, and, much
more, can relieve the country, in this important
point.

Upon these considerations I have again begged
your attention to the message of March last.
Before leaving the Capitol, consider and discuss it
among yourselves.   You are patriots and statesmen, and as such, I pray you, consider this
proposition, and at the least commend it to the
consideration of your States and people.   As you
would perpetuate popular government for the
best people in the world, I beseech you that you
do in no wise omit this.   Our common country
is in great peril, demanding the loftiest views and
boldest action to bring it speedy relief.   Once
relieved, its form of government is saved to the
world, its beloved history and cherished memories
are vindicated, and its happy future fully assured
and rendered inconceivably grand.   To you more

than to any others the privilege is given to assure
that happiness and swell that grandeur, and to
link your own names therewith forever.

LETTER TO CUTHBERT BULLITT.

July 28, 1862.

THE copy of a letter addressed to yourself by
Mr. Thomas J. Durant has been shown to me.
The writer appears to be an able, dispassionate,
and an entirely sincere man. The first part of
the letter is devoted to an effort to show that the
secession ordinance of Louisiana was adopted
against the will of the majority of the people.
This is probably true, and in that fact may be
found some instruction. Why did they allow
the ordinance to go into effect? Why did they
not exert themselves? Why stand passive and
allow themselves to be trodden down by a minority? Why did they not hold popular meetings, and have a convention of their own, to
express and enforce the true sentiments of the
State? If pre-organisation was against them,
then why not do this now, that the United States
army is present to protect them? The paralysis
— the dead palsy — of the government in this
whole struggle is, that this class of men will do noth-

18

ing for the government, nothing for themselves, except demanding that the government shall not strike its open enemies, lest they be struck by accident !

Mr. Durant complains that in various ways the relation of master and slave is disturbed by the presence of our army ; and he considers it particularly vexatious that this, in part, is done under cover of an act of Congress, while constitutional guarantees are suspended on the plea of military necessity. The truth is, that what is done and omitted about slaves, is done and omitted on the same military necessity. It is a military necessity to have men and money ; and we cannot get either in sufficient numbers or amounts if we keep from, or drive from, our lines slaves coming to them.

Mr. Durant cannot be ignorant of the pressure in this direction, nor of my efforts to hold it within bounds till he, and such as he, shall have time to help themselves.

I am not posted to speak understandingly of the police regulations of which Mr. Durant complains. If experience shows any one of them to be wrong, let them be set right. I think I can perceive in the freedom of trade which Mr. Durant urges, that he would relieve both friends and enemies from the pressure of the blockade. By this he would serve the enemy more effectively than the enemy is able to serve himself.

I do not say or believe that to serve the enemy is the purpose of Mr. Durant, or that he is conscious of any purpose other than national and patriotic ones. Still, if there were a class of men who, having no choice of sides in the contest, were anxious only to have quiet and comfort for themselves while it rages, and to fall in with the victorious side at the end of it, without loss to themselves, their advice as to the mode of conducting the contest would be precisely such as his.

He speaks of no duty — apparently thinks of none — resting upon Union men. He even thinks it injurious to the Union cause that they should be restrained in trade and passage without taking sides. They are to touch neither a sail nor a pump, — live merely as passengers (dead-heads, at that), — to be carried snug and dry throughout the storm, and safely landed right side up. Nay, more — even a mutineer is to go untouched lest these sacred passengers receive an accidental wound.

Of course the rebellion will never be suppressed in Louisiana if the professed Union men there will neither help to do it, nor permit the government to do it without their help.

Now, I think the true remedy is very different

from that suggested by Mr. Durant. It does not lie in rounding the rough angles of the war, but in removing the necessity for the war. The people of Louisiana who wish protection to person and property, have but to reach forth their hands and take it. Let them in good faith reinaugurate the national authority, and set up a State government conforming thereto under the Constitution. They know how to do it, and can have the protection of the army while doing it. The army will be withdrawn as soon as such government can dispense with its presence, and the people of the State can then, upon the old constitutional terms, govern themselves to their own liking. This is very simple and easy.

If they will not do this, if they prefer to hazard all for the sake of destroying the government, it is for them to consider whether it is probable that I will surrender the government to save them from losing all. If they decline what I suggest, you will scarcely need to ask what I will do.

What would you do in my position? Would you drop the war where it is, or would you prosecute it in future with elder-stalk squirts charged with rose-water? Would you deal lighter blows rather than heavier ones? Would you give up the contest, leaving any available means untried?

I am in no boastful mood. I shall not do more than I can ; but I shall do all I can to save the government, which is my sworn duty as well as my personal inclination. I shall do nothing in malice. What I deal with is too vast for malicious dealing.

FROM HIS LETTER TO COUNT GASPARIN.

August 4, 1862.

" . . . The moral effect was the worst of the affair before Richmond, and that has run its course downward. We are now at a stand, and shall soon be rising again, as we hope. I believe it is true that in men and material the enemy suffered more than we in that series of conflicts, while it is certain he is less able to bear it.

" With us every soldier is a man of character, and must be treated with more consideration than is customary in Europe. Hence our great army, for slighter causes than could have prevailed there, has dwindled rapidly, bringing the necessity for a new call earlier than was anticipated. We shall easily obtain the new levy, however. Be not alarmed if you shall learn that we have to draft for part of this. It seems strange even to me, but it is true, that the government is now pressed to this course by a popular demand. Thousands who wish not to personally enter the service are nevertheless anxious to pay and send substitutes, provided they can have assurance that unwilling persons, similarly situated, will be compelled to do likewise. Besides this, volunteers mostly choose to enter newly forming regiments, while drafted men can be sent to fill up old ones, wherein, man for man, they are quite doubly as valuable.

" You ask, ' Why is it that the North, with her great armies, so often is found with inferiority of numbers face to face with the armies of the South?' While I painfully know the fact, a military man, which I am not, would better answer the question. The fact, I know, has not been overlooked, and I suppose the cause of its continuance lies mainly in the other fact that the enemy holds the interior, and we the exterior lines ; and that we operate where the people convey information to the enemy, while he operates where they convey none to us. . . .

" I am very happy to know that my course has not conflicted with your judgment of propriety and policy. I can only say that I have acted upon my best convictions without selfishness or malice, and that, by the help of God, I shall continue to do so."

His Letter to Horace Greeley.

August 22, 1862.

I have just read yours of the 19th instant, addressed to myself through the " New York Tribune."

If there be in it any statements or assumptions of fact which I may know to be erroneous, I do not now and here controvert them.

If there be in it any inferences which I may believe to be falsely drawn, I do not now and here argue against them.

If there be perceptible in it an impatient and dictatorial tone, I waive it, in deference to an old friend whose heart I have always supposed to be right.

As to the policy I " seem to be pursuing," as you say, I have not meant to leave any one in doubt. I would save the Union. I would save it in the shortest way under the Constitution.

The sooner the national authority can be restored, the nearer the Union will be, — the Union as it was.

If there be those who would not save the Union unless they could at the same time save slavery, I do not agree with them.

If there be those who would not save the Union

unless they could at the same time destroy slavery, I do not agree with them.

My paramount object in this struggle is to save the Union, and not either to save or to destroy slavery.

If I could save the Union without freeing any slave, I would do it ; if I could save it by freeing all the slaves, I would do it ; and if I could save it by freeing some and leaving others alone, I would also do that.

What I do about slavery and the coloured race, I do because I believe it helps to save the Union ; and what I forbear, I forbear because I do not believe it would help to save the Union.

I shall do less whenever I shall believe that what I am doing hurts the cause ; and I shall do more whenever I shall believe doing more will help the cause.

I shall try to correct errors where shown to be errors, and I shall adopt new views as fast as they shall appear to be true views.

I have here stated my purpose according to my views of official duty, and I intend no modification of my oft-expressed personal wish that all men everywhere could be free.

From his Reply to the Chicago Committee of United Religious Denominations, urging immediate Emancipation.

September 13, 1862.

". . . I am approached with the most opposite opinions and advice, and that by religious men, who are equally certain that they represent the Divine will. I am sure that either the one or the other class is mistaken in that belief, and perhaps, in some respects, both. I hope it will not be irreverent for me to say, that if it is probable that God would reveal His will to others, on a point so connected with my duty, it might be supposed that He would reveal it directly to me ; for, unless I am more deceived in myself than I often am, it is my earnest desire to know the will of Providence in this matter. And if I can learn what it is, I will do it. These are not, however, the days of miracles, and I suppose it will be granted that I am not to expect a direct revelation. I must study the plain, physical facts of the case, ascertain what is possible, and learn what appears to be wise and right.

" The subject is difficult, and good men do not agree. For instance, four gentlemen of standing and intelligence, from New York, called as a dele-

gation on business connected with the war; but
before leaving, two of them earnestly besought
me to proclaim general emancipation, upon which
the other two at once attacked them. You also
know that the last session of Congress had a
decided majority of anti-slavery men, yet they
could not unite on this policy. And the same
is true of the religious people.

" . . . What good would a proclamation of
emancipation from me do, especially as we are
now situated? I do not want to issue a document that the whole world will see must necessarily be inoperative, like the Pope's bull against
the comet! Would my word free the slaves,
when I cannot even enforce the Constitution in
the rebel States? Is there a single court or
magistrate or individual that would be influenced
by it there? And what reason is there to think
it would have any greater effect upon the slaves
than the late law of Congress, which I approved,
and which offers protection and freedom to the
slaves of rebel masters who come within our
lines? Yet I cannot learn that that law has
caused a single slave to come over to us. And
suppose they could be induced by a proclamation
of freedom from me to throw themselves upon us,
what should we do with them? How can we feed

and care for such a multitude? General Butler wrote me a few days since that he was issuing more rations to the slaves who have rushed to him than to all the white troops under his command. They eat, and that is all; though it is true General Butler is feeding the whites also by the thousand, for it nearly amounts to a famine there. If now, the pressure of the war should call off our forces from New Orleans to defend some other point, what is to prevent the masters from reducing the blacks to slavery again? For I am told that whenever the rebels take any black prisoners, free or slave, they immediately auction them off! They did so with those they took from a boat that was aground in the Tennessee River a few days ago. And then I am very ungenerously attacked for it. For instance, when, after the late battles at and near Bull Run, an expedition went out from Washington under a flag of truce to bury the dead and bring in the wounded, and the rebels seized the blacks who went along to help, and sent them into slavery, Horace Greeley said in his paper 'that the government would probably do nothing about it.' What could I do?

" Now, then, tell me, if you please, what possible result of good would follow the issuing of such a proclamation as you desire? Understand, I raise no objections against it on legal or constitutional grounds, for, as commander-in-chief of the army and navy, in time of war I suppose I have a right to take any measures which may best subdue the enemy ; nor do I urge objections of a moral nature, in view of possible consequences of insurrection and massacre at the South. I view this matter as a practical war-measure, to be decided on according to the advantages or disadvantages it may offer to the suppression of the rebellion.''

[The committee had said that emancipation would secure us the sympathy of the world, slavery being the cause of the war. To which the President replied :]

" I admit that slavery is at the root of the rebellion, or at least its *sine qua non*. The ambition of politicians may have instigated them to act, but they would have been impotent without slavery as their instrument. I will also concede that emancipation would help us in Europe, and convince them that we are incited by something more than ambition. I grant further, that it would help somewhat at the North, though not so much, I fear, as you and those you represent, imagine. Still, some additional strength would be added in that way to the war, — and then, unquestionably, it would weaken the rebels by drawing off their labourers, which is of great importance ; but I am not so sure that we could do much with the blacks. If we were to arm them, I fear that in a few weeks the arms would be in the hands of the rebels ; and indeed, thus far, we have not had arms enough to equip our white troops. I will mention another thing, though it meet only your scorn and contempt. There are fifty thousand bayonets in the Union armies from the border slave States. It would be a serious matter if, in consequence of a proclamation such as you desire, they should go over to the rebels. I do not think they all would, — not so many indeed, as a year ago, nor as six months ago ; not so many to-day as yesterday. Every day increases their Union feeling. They are also getting their pride enlisted, and want to beat the rebels. Let me say one thing more : I think you should admit that we already have an important principle to rally and unite the people, in the fact that constitutional government is at stake. This is a fundamental idea, going down about as deep as anything.

" Do not misunderstand me because I have mentioned these objections. They indicate the difficulties that have thus far prevented my action in some such way as you desire. I have not decided against a proclamation of liberty to the slaves, but hold the matter under advisement. And I can assure you that the subject is on my mind by day and night, more than any other. Whatever shall appear to be God's will, I will do. I trust that in the freedom with which I have canvassed your views, I have not in any respect injured your feelings."

His Order to remember and keep the Sabbath Day.

November 15, 1862.

THE President, commander-in-chief of the army and navy, desires and enjoins the orderly observance of the Sabbath by the officers and men in the military and naval service. The importance for man and beast of the prescribed weekly rest, the sacred rights of Christian soldiers and sailors, a becoming deference to the best sentiment of a Christian people, and a due regard for the Divine will demand that Sunday labour in the army and navy be reduced to the measure of strict necessity. The discipline and character of the national forces should not suffer, nor the cause they defend be imperilled, by the profanation of the day or name of the Most High.   " At this time of public distress," adopting the words of Washington, in 1776, "men may find enough to do in the service of God and their country, without abandoning themselves to vice and immorality." The first general order issued by the Father of his Country, after the Declaration of Independence, indicates the spirit in which our institutions were founded and should ever be defended. "The general hopes and trusts that every officer and man will endeavour to live and act as becomes a Christian soldier, defending the dearest rights and liberties of his country."

FROM THE ANNUAL MESSAGE TO CONGRESS.

December 1, 1862.

"SINCE your last annual assembling, another year of health and bountiful harvests has passed ; and while it has not pleased the Almighty to bless us with a return of peace, we can but press on, guided by the best light He gives us, trusting that in His own good time and wise way, all will yet be well.

". . . If the condition of our relations with other nations is less gratifying than it has usually been at former periods, it is certainly more satisfactory than a nation so unhappily distracted as we are, might reasonably have apprehended.   In the month of June last, there were some grounds to expect that the maritime powers, which, at the beginning of our domestic difficulties, so unwisely and unnecessarily, as we think, recognised the insurgents as a belligerent, would soon recede from that position, which has proved only less injurious to themselves than to our own country. But the temporary reverses which afterward befell the national arms, and which were exaggerated by our own disloyal citizens abroad, have hitherto delayed that act of simple justice.

" The Civil War, which has so radically changed for the moment the occupations and habits of the American people, has necessarily disturbed the social condition and affected very deeply the prosperity of the nations with which we have carried on a commerce that has been steadily increasing throughout a period of half a century. It has, at the same time, excited political ambitions and apprehensions which have produced a profound agitation throughout the civilised world. In this unusual agitation we have forborne from taking part in any controversy between foreign States, and between parties or factions in such States.   We have attempted no propagandism and acknowledged no revolution. But we have left to every nation the exclusive conduct and management of its own affairs. Our struggle has been, of course, contemplated by foreign nations with reference less to its own merits than to its supposed and often exaggerated effects and consequences resulting to those nations themselves. Nevertheless, complaint on the part of this government, even if it were just, would certainly be unwise.

". . . The condition of the finances will claim your most diligent consideration. The vast expenditures incident to the military and naval operations required for the suppression of the rebellion, have hitherto been met with a promptitude and certainty unusual in similar circumstances, and the public credit has been fully maintained.

". . . A nation may be said to consist of its territory, its people, and its laws. The territory is the only part which is of certain durability. 'One generation passeth away, and another generation cometh, but the earth abideth forever.' It is of the first importance to duly consider and estimate this ever-enduring part. That portion of the earth's surface which is owned and inhabited by the people of the United States is well adapted to be the home of one national family,

19

and it is not well adapted for two or more.   Its
vast extent and its variety of climate and productions are of advantage in this age for one
people, whatever they might have been in former
ages.   Steam, telegraphs, and intelligence have
brought these to be an advantageous combination
for one united people.

"In the inaugural address I briefly pointed out
the total inadequacy of disunion as a remedy for
the differences between the people of the two sections.   [Here several paragraphs from the inaugural address were repeated.]

". . . There is no line, straight or crooked,
suitable for a national boundary, upon which to
divide.   Trace through from east to west upon
the line between the free and the slave country,
and we shall find a little more than one third of
its length are rivers, easy to be crossed, and populated, or soon to be populated, thickly upon
both sides; while nearly all its remaining length
are merely surveyors' lines, over which people
may walk back and forth without any consciousness of their presence.   No part of this line can
be made any more difficult to pass, by writing it
down on paper or parchment as a national boundary.   The fact of separation, if it comes, gives
up, on the part of the seceding section, the fugitive-

slave clause, along with all other constitutional obligations upon the section seceded from, while I should expect no treaty stipulation would be ever made to take its place.

" But there is another difficulty. The great interior region bounded east by the Alleghanies, north by the British dominions, west by the Rocky Mountains, and south by the line along which the culture of corn and cotton meets, . . . already has above ten millions of people, and will have fifty millions within fifty years, if not prevented by any political folly or mistake. It contains more than one-third of the country owned by the United States, — certainly more than one million of square miles. Once half as populous as Massachusetts already is, and it would have more than seventy-five millions of people. A glance at the map shows that, territorially speaking, it is the great body of the republic. The other parts are but marginal borders to it. . . . In the production of provisions, grains, grasses, and all which proceed from them, this great interior region is naturally one of the most important in the world. Ascertain from the statistics the small proportion of the region which has, as yet, been brought into cultivation, and also the large and rapidly increasing amount of its products, and we shall be overwhelmed with the magnitude of the prospect presented. And yet this region has no sea-coast, touches no ocean anywhere. As part of one nation, its people now find, and may forever find, their way to Europe by New York, to South America and Africa by New Orleans, and to Asia by San Francisco. But separate our common country into two nations, as designed by the present rebellion, and every man of this great interior region is thereby cut off from one or more of these outlets, — not perhaps by a physical barrier, but by embarrassing and onerous trade regulations.

" . . . These outlets, east, west, and south, are indispensable to the well-being of the people inhabiting, and to inhabit, this vast interior region. Which of the three may be the best, is no proper question. All are better than either; and all of right belong to that people and their successors forever. True to themselves, they will not ask where a line of separation shall be, but will vow rather that there shall be no such line. Nor are the marginal regions less interested in these communications to and through them to the great outside world. They too, and each of them, must have access to this Egypt of the west, without paying toll at the crossing of any national boundary.

" Our national strife springs not from our permanent part, not from the land we inhabit, not from our national homestead. There is no possible severing of this but would multiply and not mitigate evils among us. In all its adaptations and aptitudes, it demands union and abhors separation. In fact, it would ere long force reunion, however much of blood and treasure the separation might have cost.

" . . . Fellow-citizens, we cannot escape history. We of this Congress and this Administration will be remembered in spite of ourselves. No personal significance or insignificance can spare one or another of us. The fiery trial through which we pass will light us down, in honour or dishonour, to the latest generation. We say we are for the Union. The world will not forget that we say this. We know how to save the Union. The world knows we do know how to save it. We, even we here, hold the power and bear the responsibility. In giving freedom to the slave, we assure freedom to the free, — honourable alike in what we give and what we preserve. We shall nobly save or meanly lose the last, best hope of earth. Other means may succeed ; this could not fail. The way is plain, peaceful, generous, just, — a way which, if followed, the world will forever applaud, and God must forever bless."

DRAFT OF THE PROCLAMATION OF EMANCIPATION
AS SUBMITTED TO THE CABINET FOR FINAL
REVISION.

December 30, 1862.

Now therefore, I, Abraham Lincoln, President
of the United States, by virtue of the power in
me vested as commander-in-chief of the army
and navy of the United States, in time of actual
armed rebellion against the authority and government of the United States, and as a proper and
necessary war-measure for suppressing said rebellion, do, on this first day of January, in the year
of our Lord one thousand eight hundred and
sixty-three, and in accordance with my intention
so to do, publicly proclaimed for one hundred
days as aforesaid, order and designate as the
States and parts of States in which the people
thereof, respectively, are this day in rebellion
against the United States, the following, to wit :

[Here follow the States and counties named.]

And by virtue of the power, and for the purpose aforesaid, I do order and declare that all
persons held as slaves within said designated
States and parts of States are, and henceforward
forever shall be free ; and that the Executive
Government of the United States, including the
military and naval authorities thereof, will recog-

nise and maintain the freedom of said persons, and will do no act or acts to repress said persons or any of them, in any suitable efforts they may make for their actual freedom ; and I hereby appeal to the people so declared to be free, to abstain from all disorder, tumult, and violence, unless in necessary self-defence, and in all cases, when allowed, to labour faithfully for wages.

And I further declare and make known, that such persons of suitable condition will be received into the armed service of the United States, to garrison and defend forts, positions, stations, and other places, and to man vessels of all sorts in said service.

The Proclamation of Emancipation.

January 1, 1863.

Whereas, on the twenty-second day of September, in the year of our Lord one thousand eight hundred and sixty-two, a proclamation was issued by the President of the United States, containing among other things the following, to wit :

" That on the first day of January, in the year of our Lord one thousand eight hundred and sixty-three, all persons held as slaves, within any State or designated part of a State, the people

whereof shall then be in rebellion against the
United States, shall be then, thenceforward and
forever, free ; and the executive government of the
United States, including the military and naval
authority thereof, will recognise and maintain the
freedom of such persons, and will do no act or
acts to repress such persons, or any of them, in any
efforts they may make for their actual freedom.

" That the Executive will, on the first day of
January aforesaid, by proclamation, designate the
States and parts of States, if any, in which the
people thereof, respectively, shall be then in rebellion against the United States ; and the fact
that any State, or the people thereof, shall, on
that day, be in good faith represented in the
Congress of the United States, by members
chosen thereto at elections wherein a majority
of the qualified voters of such State shall have
participated, shall, in the absence of strong coun-
tervailing testimony, be deemed conclusive evidence that such State and the people thereof,
are not then in rebellion against the United
States."

Now therefore, I, Abraham Lincoln, President
of the United States, by virtue of the power in me
vested as commander-in-chief of the army and
navy of the United States, in time of actual armed

rebellion against the authority and government of the United States, and as a fit and necessary war-measure for suppressing said rebellion, do, on this first day of January, in the year of our Lord one thousand eight hundred and sixty-three, and in accordance with my purpose so to do, publicly proclaimed for the full period of one hundred days from the day first above mentioned, order and designate as the States and parts of States wherein the people thereof respectively are this day in rebellion against the United States, the following, to wit :

[Here follows the enumeration.]

And by virtue of the power and for the purpose aforesaid, I do order and declare that all persons held as slaves within said designated States and parts of States are, and henceforward shall be, free ; and that the executive government of the United States, including the military and naval authorities thereof, will recognise and maintain the freedom of said persons.

And I hereby enjoin upon the people so declared to be free, to abstain from all violence, unless in necessary self-defence ; and I recommend to them that in all cases when allowed, they labour faithfully for reasonable wages.

And I further declare and make known, that

such persons of suitable condition will be received into the armed service of the United States, to garrison forts, positions, stations, and other places, and to man vessels of all sorts in said service.

And upon this act, sincerely believed to be an act of justice, warranted by the Constitution upon military necessity, I invoke the considerate judgment of mankind and the gracious favour of Almighty God.

FROM HIS MESSAGE TO CONGRESS.

January 17, 1863.

" . . . While giving this approval, I think it my duty to express my sincere regret that it has been found necessary to authorise so large an additional issue of United States notes, when this circulation and that of the suspended banks together have become already so redundant as to increase prices beyond real values, thereby augmenting the cost of living to the injury of labour, and the cost of supplies to the injury of the whole country. It seems very plain that the continued issues of United States notes, without any check to the issues of suspended banks, and without adequate provision for the raising of money by loans, and for funding the issues so as to keep them within due limits, must soon produce disastrous consequences; and this matter appears to me so important, that I feel bound to avail myself of this occasion to ask the special attention of Congress to it.

"That Congress has power to regulate the currency of the country can hardly admit of a doubt, and that a judicious measure to prevent the deterioration of this currency by a reasonable taxation of bank circulation, or otherwise, is needed, seems equally clear. Independently of this general consideration, it would be unjust to the people at large to exempt banks enjoying the special privilege of circulation from their just proportion of the public burdens.

"In order to raise money by way of loans most easily and cheaply, it is clearly necessary to give every possible support to the public credit. To that end, a uniform currency in which taxes, subscriptions to loans, and all other ordinary public dues, as well as all private, may be paid, is almost if not quite indispensable. Such a currency can be furnished by banking associations, organised under a general act of Congress, as suggested in my message at the beginning of the present session. The securing of this circulation

by a pledge of United States bonds, as therein
suggested, would still further facilitate loans, by
increasing the present and causing a future demand for such bonds.

". . . By such measures, in my opinion, will
payment be most certainly secured, not only to
the army and navy, but to all honest creditors
of the government, and satisfactory provision
made for future demands upon the treasury."

HIS LETTER TO THE WORKING-MEN OF MAN-
CHESTER, ENGLAND.

January 19, 1863.

I HAVE the honour to acknowledge the receipt of
the address and resolutions which you sent me on
the eve of the New Year.   When I came, on the
fourth of March, 1861, through a free and constitutional election, to preside in the government
of the United States, the country was found at
the verge of civil war.   Whatever might have
been the cause, or whosesoever the fault, one
duty paramount to all others was before me ;
namely, to maintain and preserve at once the
Constitution and the integrity of the Federal Republic.   A conscientious purpose to perform this

duty is the key to all the measures of administration which have been, and to all which will hereafter be, pursued. Under our frame of government and by my official oath, I could not depart from this purpose if I would. It is not always in the power of governments to enlarge or restrict the scope of moral results which follow the policies that they may deem it necessary for the public safety from time to time to adopt.

I have understood well that the duty of self-preservation rests solely with the American people ; but I have at the same time been aware that favour or disfavour of foreign nations might have a material influence in enlarging or prolonging the struggle with disloyal men in which the country is engaged. A fair examination of history has served to authorise a belief that the past actions and influences of the United States were generally regarded as having been beneficial toward mankind. I have therefore reckoned upon the forbearance of nations. Circumstances, to some of which you kindly allude, induce me especially to expect that if justice and good faith should be practised by the United States, they would encounter no hostile influence on the part of Great Britain. It is now a pleasant duty to acknowledge the demonstration you have given of your desire that a spirit of amity and peace toward this country may prevail in the councils of your Queen, who is respected and esteemed in your own country only more than she is by the kindred nation which has its home on this side of the Atlantic.

I know and deeply deplore the sufferings which the working-men at Manchester, and in all Europe, are called to endure in this crisis. It has been often and studiously represented that the attempt to overthrow this government, which was built upon the foundation of human rights, and to substitute for it one which should rest exclusively on the basis of human slavery, was likely to obtain the favour of Europe. Through the action of our disloyal citizens, the working-men of Europe have been subjected to severe trials, for the purpose of forcing their sanction to that attempt. Under the circumstances, I cannot but regard your decisive utterances upon the question as an instance of sublime Christian heroism, which has not been surpassed in any age or in any country. It is indeed an energetic and reinspiring assurance of the inherent power of truth, and of the ultimate and universal triumph of justice, humanity, and freedom. I do not doubt that the sentiments you have expressed will be sustained by your great nation; and, on the other hand, I have no hesitation in assuring you that they will excite admiration, esteem, and the most reciprocal feelings of friendship among the American people. I hail this interchange of sentiment, therefore, as an augury that whatever else may happen, whatever misfortune may befall your country or my own, the peace and friendship which now exist between the two nations will be, as it shall be my desire to make them, perpetual.

His Letter to General Hooker.

January 26, 1863.

General: I have placed you at the head of the army of the Potomac. Of course I have done this upon what appear to me to be sufficient reasons, and yet I think it best for you to know that there are some things in regard to which I am not quite satisfied with you. I believe you to be a brave and skilful soldier, which of course I like. I also believe you do not mix politics with your profession, in which you are right. You have confidence in yourself, which is a valuable if not an indispensable quality. You are ambitious, which, within reasonable bounds, does good rather than harm ; but I think that during General Burnside's command of the army you have taken counsel of your ambition, and thwarted him as much as you could, — in which you did a great wrong to the country, and to a most meritorious and honourable brother officer.   I have heard, in such a way as to believe it, of your recently saying that the army and the government needed a dictator.   Of course it was not for this, but in spite of it, that I have given you the command. Only those generals who gain successes can set up dictators.   What I now ask of you is military success, and I will risk the dictatorship.   The government will support you to the utmost of its ability, which is neither more nor less than it has done and will do for all commanders.   I much fear that the spirit which you have aided to infuse into the army, of criticising their commander and withholding confidence from him, will now turn upon you.   I shall assist you as far as I can to put it down.   Neither you nor Napoleon, if he were alive again, could get any good out of an army while such a spirit prevails in it.   And now beware of rashness.   Beware of rashness, but with energy and sleepless vigilance, go forward and give us victories.

LETTER TO REV. ALEXANDER REED.

February 22, 1863.

YOUR note by which you, as general superintendent of the United States Christian Commission, invite me to preside at a meeting to be this day held at the hall of the House of Representatives in this city, is received.

While, for reasons which I deem sufficient, I must decline to preside, I cannot withhold my approval of the meeting and its worthy objects. Whatever shall be sincerely, and in God's name, devised for the good of the soldier and seaman in their hard spheres of duty, can scarcely fail to be blessed. And whatever shall tend to turn our thoughts from the unreasoning and uncharitable passions, prejudices, and jealousies incident to a great national trouble such as ours, and to fix them upon the vast and long-enduring consequences, for weal or for woe, which are to result from the struggle, and especially to strengthen our reliance on the Supreme Being for the final triumph of the right, cannot but be well for us all.

The birthday of Washington and the Christian Sabbath, coinciding this year, and suggesting together the highest interests of this life and of that to come, is most propitious for the meeting proposed.

20

From his Reply to the Presbyterian Clergymen.

May, 1863.

"It has been my happiness to receive testimonies of a similar nature from, I believe, all denominations of Christians. They are all loyal, but perhaps not in the same degree, or in the same numbers; but I think they all claim to be loyal. This to me is most gratifying, because from the beginning I saw that the issue of our great struggle depended on the Divine interposition and favour. If we had that, all would be well. The proportions of this rebellion were not for a long time understood. I saw that it involved the greatest difficulties, and would call forth all the powers of the country. The end is not yet.

"The point made in your paper is well taken as to the 'government' and 'the administration,' in whose hands are these interests. I fully appreciate its correctness and justice. In my administration I may have committed some errors. It would be indeed remarkable if I had not. I have acted according to my best judgment in every case. The views expressed by the committee accord with my own; and on this principle 'the government' is to be supported, though 'the administration' may not in every case wisely act. As a pilot I have used my best exertions to keep afloat our ship of state, and shall be glad to resign my trust at the appointed time to another pilot, more skilful and successful than I may prove. In every case and at all hazards, the government must be perpetuated. Relying as I do upon the Almighty Power, and encouraged as I am by the resolutions which you have just read, with the support which I receive from Christian men, I shall not hesitate to use all the means at my control to secure the termination of this rebellion, and will hope for success. . . ."

LETTER TO ERASTUS CORNING AND OTHERS.

June 12, 1863.

[THIS letter is the President's answer to the resolutions of a Democratic convention which assert the loyalty of its members, but censure Mr. Lincoln for his suspension of the writ of habeas corpus, and for approving military arrests in places not actually in rebellion. The reply is an unanswerable justification of his acts. As a legal argument it is conclusive, and as a specimen of English composition it is clear, logical, and beautiful. Its length (about 4500 words) prevents the insertion here of the entire document. To take an extract from it would be like removing a stone from the granite wall of a noble edifice : it would deface the beauty and weaken the strength of the wall, without giving any adequate idea of the building. No selection from it is therefore attempted.]

From his Reply to the Resolutions of the Democratic State Convention of Ohio.

June 29, 1863.

[C. L. Vallandigham, a member of the last Congress from Ohio, and a man of misdirected ability, had by his speeches in Congress and elsewhere promoted the rebellion up to the verge of treason. On the 19th of May, 1863, the President ordered General Canby to put Vallandigham beyond the lines, and if he returned, to arrest and imprison him. The Democratic Convention of Ohio then nominated him for governor, and passed and sent resolutions to the President which, while declaring its purpose to sustain the National Union by all constitutional means, reasserted the objections of the Corning letter, and protested against the arrest and deportation of Vallandigham as unlawful and an insult to Ohio. In this reply, among other things, the President said :]

" You claim that men may, if they choose, embarrass those whose duty it is to combat a giant rebellion, and then be dealt with in turn as if there were no rebellion. The Constitution itself rejects this view. The military arrests and detentions which have been made, including those of Mr. Vallandigham, which are not different in principle from the others, have been made for prevention and not for punishment, — as injunctions to stay injury, as proceedings to keep the peace.

" . . . I am unable to perceive an insult to Ohio in the case of Mr. Vallandigham. Quite surely nothing of the sort was or is intended. I was wholly unaware that Mr. Vallandigham was, at the time of his arrest, a candidate for the Democratic nomination for governor until so informed by your reading to me the resolutions of the convention. I am grateful to the State of Ohio for many things, especially for the brave soldiers and officers she has given in the present national trial to the armies of the Union.

" . . . We all know that combinations, armed in some instances, to resist the arrest of deserters began several months ago ; that more recently the like has appeared in resistance to the enrolment preparatory to the draft ; and that quite a number of assassinations have occurred from the same animus. These had to be met by military force,

and this again has led to bloodshed and death. And now, under a sense of responsibility more weighty and enduring than any which is merely official, I solemnly declare my belief that this hindrance of the military, including maiming and murder, is due to the course in which Mr. Vallandigham has been engaged, in a greater degree than to any other cause ; and it is due to him personally in a greater degree than to any other man.

"These things have been notorious, known to all, and of course known to Mr. Vallandigham. Perhaps I would not be wrong to say they originated with his special friends and adherents. With perfect knowledge of them, he has frequently, if not constantly, made speeches in Congress and before popular assemblies ; and if it can be shown that, with these things staring him in the face, he has ever uttered a word of rebuke or counsel against them, it will be a fact greatly in his favour with me, and one of which I am as yet totally ignorant.

" . . . With all this before their eyes, the convention you represent have nominated Mr. Vallandigham for governor of Ohio, and both they and you have declared the purpose to sustain the National Union by all constitutional means.   But of course they and you in common reserve to yourselves to decide what are constitutional means; and, unlike the Albany meeting, you omit to state or intimate that in your opinion an army is a constitutional means of saving the Union against a rebellion, or even to intimate that you are conscious of an existing rebellion being in progress with the avowed object of destroying that very Union. At the same time your nominee for governor, in whose behalf you appeal, is known to you and to the world to declare against the use of an army to suppress the rebellion. Your own attitude, therefore, encourages desertion, resistance to the draft and the like, because it teaches those who incline to desert and to escape the draft to believe it is your purpose to protect them, and to hope that you will become strong enough to do so.

"After a short personal intercourse with you, gentlemen, I cannot say that you desire this effect to follow your attitude; but I assure you that both friends and enemies of the Union look upon it in this light. It is a substantial hope, and by consequence a real strength, to the enemy. If it is a false hope, and one you would willingly dispel, I will make the way exceedingly easy.

"I send you duplicates of this letter, in order that you or a majority of you, may, if you choose, indorse your names upon one of them, and return it thus indorsed to me, with the understanding that those signing are thereby committed to the following propositions, and to nothing else : —

"'1. That there is now a rebellion in the United States, the object and tendency of which is to destroy the National Union ; and that in your opinion an army and navy are constitutional means for suppressing that rebellion ;

"'2. That no one of you will do anything which, in his own judgment, will tend to hinder the increase, or favour the decrease, or lessen the efficiency of the army or navy while engaged in the effort to suppress that rebellion ; and

"'3. That each of you will, in his sphere, do all he can to have the officers, soldiers, and seamen of the army and navy, while engaged in the effort to suppress the rebellion, paid, fed, clad, and otherwise well supported and provided for.

"'And with the further understanding that upon receiving the letter and names thus indorsed, I will cause them to be published, which publication shall be, within itself, a revocation of the order in relation to Mr. Vallandigham.'

"It will not escape observation that I consent to the release of Mr. Vallandigham upon terms not embracing any pledge from him or from others

as to what he will or will not do. I do this because he is not present to speak for himself, or to
authorise others to speak for him ; and because I
should expect that on his returning he would not
put himself practically in antagonism with the
position of his friends. But I do it chiefly because I thereby prevail on other influential gentlemen of Ohio to so define their position as to
be of immense value to the army, thus more
than compensating for the consequences of any
mistake in allowing Mr. Vallandigham to return ;
so that, on the whole, the public safety will not
have suffered by it. Still, in regard to Mr. Vallandigham and all others, I must hereafter, as
heretofore, do so much as the public safety may
seem to require."

THE LETTER TO JAMES C. CONKLING.

August 26, 1863.

YOUR letter inviting me to attend a mass meeting of unconditional Union men, to be held at
the capital of Illinois on the third day of September, has been received. It would be very
agreeable to me to thus meet my old friends at
my own home, but I cannot just now be absent
from here so long as a visit there would require.

The meeting is to be of all those who maintain unconditional devotion to the Union; and I am sure my old political friends will thank me for tendering, as I do, the nation's gratitude to those and other noble men whom no partisan malice or partisan hope can make false to the nation's life.

There are those who are dissatisfied with me. To such I would say: You desire peace, and you blame me that we do not have it. But how can we attain it? There are but three conceivable ways. First, to suppress the rebellion by force of arms. This I am trying to do. Are you for it? If you are, so far we are agreed. If you are not for it, a second way is to give up the Union. I am against this. Are you for it? If you are, you should say so plainly. If you are not for force, nor yet for dissolution, there only remains some imaginable compromise. I do not believe any compromise embracing the maintenance of the Union is now possible. All I learn leads to a directly opposite belief. The strength of the rebellion is its military, its army. That army dominates all the country and all the people within its range. Any offer of terms made by any man or men within that range, in opposition to that army, is simply nothing for the present, because such man or men have no power whatever to enforce their side of a compromise, if one were made with them.

To illustrate : Suppose refugees from the South and peace men of the North get together in convention, and frame and proclaim a compromise embracing a restoration of the Union. In what way can that compromise be used to keep Lee's army out of Pennsylvania? Meade's army can keep Lee's out of Pennsylvania, and, I think, can ultimately drive it out of existence. But no paper compromise, to which the controllers of Lee's army are not agreed, can at all affect that army. In an effort at such compromise we should waste time which the enemy would improve to our disadvantage ; and that would be all. A compromise, to be effective, must be made either with those who control the rebel army, or with the people first liberated from the domination of that army by the success of our own army. Now, allow me to assure you that no word or intimation from that rebel army, or from any of the men controlling it, in relation to any peace compromise, has ever come to my knowledge or belief. All charges and insinuations to the contrary are deceptive and groundless. And I promise you that if any such proposition shall hereafter come, it shall not be rejected and kept a secret from you. I freely acknowledge myself the servant of the people, according to the bond of service, — the United States Constitution, — and that, as such, I am responsible to them.

But to be plain. You are dissatisfied with me about the negro. Quite likely there is a difference of opinion between you and myself upon that subject. I certainly wish that all men could be free, while I suppose you do not. Yet I have neither adopted nor proposed any measure which is not consistent with even your views, provided you are for the Union. I suggested compensated emancipation, to which you replied, you wished not to be taxed to buy negroes. But I had not asked you to be taxed to buy negroes, except in such way as to save you from greater taxation to save the Union exclusively by other means.

You dislike the Emancipation Proclamation, and perhaps would have it retracted. You say it is unconstitutional. I think differently. I think the Constitution invests its commander-in-chief with the law of war in time of war. The most that can be said — if so much — is that slaves are property. Is there, has there ever been, any question that, by the law of war, property, both of enemies and friends, may be taken when needed? And is it not needed whenever taking it helps us or hurts the enemy? Armies the world over destroy enemies' property when they cannot use it, and even destroy their own to keep it from the enemy. Civilised belligerents do all in their power to help themselves or hurt the enemy, except a few things regarded as barbarous or cruel. Among the exceptions are the massacre of vanquished foes and non-combatants, male and female.

But the proclamation, as law, either is valid or is not valid. If it is not valid, it needs no retraction. If it is valid, it cannot be retracted any more than the dead can be brought to life. Some of you profess to think its retraction would operate favourably for the Union. Why better after the retraction than before the issue? There was more than a year and a half of trial to suppress the rebellion before the proclamation issued, the last one hundred days of which passed under an explicit notice that it was coming, unless averted by those in revolt returning to their allegiance. The war has certainly progressed as favourably for us since the issue of the proclamation as before. I know, as fully as one can know the opinions of others, that some of the commanders of our armies in the field who have given us our most important successes, believe the emancipation policy and the use of coloured troops constitute the heaviest blow yet dealt to the rebellion, and that at least one of these important successes could not have been achieved when it was but for the aid of black soldiers. Among the commanders holding these views are some who have never had any affinity with what is called Abolitionism or with Republican party politics, but who hold them purely as military opinions. I submit these opinions as being entitled to some weight against the objections often urged, that emancipation and arming the blacks are unwise as military measures, and were not adopted as such in good faith.

You say you will not fight to free negroes. Some of them seem willing to fight for you; but no matter. Fight you, then, exclusively to save the Union. I issued the proclamation on purpose to aid you in saving the Union. Whenever you shall have conquered all resistance to the Union, if I shall urge you to continue fighting, it will be an apt time then for you to declare you will not fight to free negroes.

I thought that in your struggle for the Union, to whatever extent the negroes should cease helping the enemy, to that extent it weakened the enemy in his resistance to you. Do you think differently? I thought that whatever negroes could be got to do as soldiers leaves just so much less for white soldiers to do in saving the Union. Does it appear otherwise to you? But negroes, like other people, act upon motives. Why should they do anything for us, if we will do nothing for them? If they stake their lives for us, they must be prompted by the strongest motive, even the promise of freedom. And the promise being made, must be kept.

The signs look better. The Father of Waters again goes unvexed to the sea. Thanks to the great Northwest for it. Nor yet wholly to them. Three hundred miles up they met New England, Empire, Keystone, and Jersey hewing their way right and left. The sunny South, too, in more colours than one, also lent a hand. On the spot, their part of the history was jotted down in black and white. The job was a great national one, and let none be banned who bore an honourable part in it. And while those who cleared the great river may well be proud, even that is not all. It is hard to say that anything has been more bravely and well done than at Antietam, Murfreesboro, Gettysburg, and on many fields of lesser note. Nor must Uncle Sam's web-feet be forgotten. At all the watery margins they have been present. Not only on the deep sea, the broad bay, and the rapid river, but also up the narrow, muddy bayou, and wherever the ground was a little damp, they have been and made their tracks. Thanks to all, — for the great Republic, for the principle it lives by and keeps alive, for man's vast future, — thanks to all.

Peace does not appear so distant as it did. I hope it will come soon, and come to stay; and so come as to be worth the keeping in all future time. It will then have been proved that among freemen there can be no successful appeal from the ballot to the bullet, and that they who take such appeal are sure to lose their case and pay the cost. And then there will be some black men who can remember that with silent tongue, and clenched teeth, and steady eye, and well-poised bayonet, they have helped mankind on to this great consummation, while I fear there will be some white ones unable to forget that with malignant heart and deceitful speech they strove to hinder it.

Still, let us not be over-sanguine of a speedy, final triumph. Let us be quite sober. Let us diligently apply the means, never doubting that a just God, in His own good time, will give us the rightful result.

His Proclamation for a Day of Thanksgiving.

October 3, 1863.

THE year that is drawing toward its close has been filled with the blessings of fruitful fields and healthful skies. To these bounties, which are so constantly enjoyed that we are prone to forget the source from which they come, others have been added, which are of so extraordinary a nature that they cannot fail to penetrate and soften the heart which is habitually insensible to the ever-watchful providence of Almighty God.

In the midst of a civil war of unequalled magnitude and severity, which has sometimes seemed to foreign States to invite and provoke their aggressions, peace has been preserved with all nations, order has been maintained, the laws have been respected and obeyed, and harmony has prevailed everywhere, except in the theatre of military conflict; while that theatre has been greatly contracted by the advancing armies and navies of the Union.

Needful diversions of wealth and strength from the fields of peaceful industry to the national defence have not arrested the plough, the shuttle, or the ship; the axe has enlarged the borders of our settlements, and the mines, as well of iron and

21

coal as of the precious metals, have yielded even more abundantly than heretofore. Population has steadily increased, notwithstanding the waste that has been made in the camp, the siege, and the battle-field ; and the country, rejoicing in the consciousness of augmented strength and vigour, is permitted to expect continuance of years with large increase of freedom.

No human counsel hath devised, nor hath any mortal hand worked out these great things. They are the gracious gifts of the Most High God, who, while dealing with us in anger for our sins, hath nevertheless remembered mercy.

It has seemed to me fit and proper that they should be solemnly, reverently, and gratefully acknowledged as with one heart and one voice by the whole American people. I do, therefore, invite my fellow-citizens in every part of the United States, and also those who are at sea, and those sojourning in foreign lands, to set apart and observe the last Thursday of November next as a day of thanksgiving and praise to our beneficent Father who dwelleth in the heavens. And I recommend to them that, while offering up the ascriptions justly due to Him for such singular deliverances and blessings, they do also, with humble penitence for our national perverseness and disobedience, commend to his tender care all those who have become widows, orphans, mourners, or sufferers in the lamentable civil strife in which we are unavoidably engaged, and fervently implore the interposition of the Almighty Hand to heal the wounds of the nation, and to restore it, as soon as may be consistent with the Divine purposes, to the full enjoyment of peace, harmony, tranquillity, and union.

REMARKS AT THE DEDICATION OF THE NATIONAL CEMETERY AT GETTYSBURG.

November 19, 1863.

[NOTE. — Is the address at Gettysburg, or his second inaugural, the best example of English composition from the pen of Abraham Lincoln? Upon this question, critics may well differ. Mr. Lincoln himself, in his letter to Thurlow Weed, of March 15, 1865, wrote that he expected the latter (the second inaugural) to wear as well as — perhaps better than — anything he had produced. But he thought it was not immediately popular, for men are not flattered by being shown that there has been a difference of opinion between the Almighty and them.

Neither of these examples could have been written by one who was not a master of English composition. But there is a dignity, a simplicity, and a completeness in the address at Gettysburg which will make it noted as long as the language endures.]

FOURSCORE and seven years ago our fathers brought forth upon this continent a new nation, conceived in liberty, and dedicated to the proposition that all men are created equal.

Now we are engaged in a great civil war, testing whether that nation, or any nation so conceived and so dedicated, can long endure. We are met on a great battle-field of that war. We have come to dedicate a portion of that field as a final resting-place for those who here gave their lives that that nation might live. It is altogether fitting and proper that we should do this.

But in a larger sense we cannot dedicate, we cannot consecrate, we cannot hallow this ground. The brave men, living and dead, who struggled here, have consecrated it far above our power to add or detract. The world will little note nor long remember what we say here, but it can never forget what they did here. It is for us, the living, rather, to be dedicated here to the unfinished work which they who fought here have thus far so nobly advanced. It is rather for us to be here dedicated to the great task remaining before us; that from these honoured dead we take increased devotion to that cause for which they gave the last full measure of devotion; that we here highly resolve that these dead shall not have died in vain; that this nation, under God, shall have a new birth of freedom; and that government of the people, by the people, and for the people, shall not perish from the earth.

From the Annual Message to Congress.

December 8, 1863.

" . . . When Congress assembled a year ago, the war had already lasted nearly twenty months, and there had been many conflicts on both land and sea, with varying results. The rebellion had been pressed back into reduced limits; yet the tone of public feeling and opinion at home and abroad was not satisfactory. With other signs, the popular elections then just past indicated uneasiness among ourselves; while, amid much that was cold and menacing, the kindest words coming from Europe were uttered in accents of pity that we were too blind to surrender a hopeless cause. Our commerce was suffering greatly from a few vessels built upon and furnished from foreign shores, and we were threatened with such additions from the same quarter as would sweep our trade from the seas and raise our blockade. We had failed to elicit from European governments anything hopeful upon this subject. The preliminary Emancipation Proclamation, issued in September, was running its assigned period to the beginning of the new year. A month later the final proclamation came, including the announcement that coloured men of suitable condition would be received into the war service. The policy of emancipation and of employing black soldiers gave to the future a new aspect, about which hope and fear and doubt contended in uncertain conflict. According to our political system, as a matter of civil administration, the general government had no lawful power to effect emancipation in any State, and for a long time it had been hoped that the rebellion could be suppressed without resorting to it as a military measure. It was all the while deemed possible that the necessity for it might come, and that, if it should, the crisis of the contest would then be presented. It came, and, as was anticipated, was followed by dark and doubtful days. Eleven months having now passed, we are permitted to take another

review. The rebel borders are pressed still farther back, and by the complete opening of the
Mississippi, the country dominated by the rebellion is divided into distinct parts, with no practical communication between them. Tennessee
and Arkansas have been substantially cleared of
insurgent control, and influential citizens in each,
owners of slaves and advocates of slavery at the
beginning of the rebellion, now declare openly
for emancipation in their respective States. Of
those States not included in the Emancipation
Proclamation, Maryland and Missouri, neither of
which three years ago would tolerate any restraint
upon the extension of slavery into new Territories,
only dispute now as to the best mode of removing
it within their own limits.

" Of those who were slaves at the beginning of
the rebellion, full one hundred thousand are now
in the United States military service, about one
half of which number actually bear arms in the
ranks ; thus giving the double advantage of taking
so much labour from the insurgent cause and sup-
plying the places which otherwise must be filled
with so many white men. So far as tested, it is
difficult to say they are not as good soldiers as
any. No servile insurrection or tendency to violence or cruelty has marked the measures of eman-

cipation and arming the blacks. These measures have been much discussed in foreign countries, and contemporary with such discussion the tone of public sentiment there is much improved. At home the same measures have been fully discussed, supported, criticised, and denounced, and the annual elections following are highly encouraging to those whose official duty it is to bear the country through this great trial. Thus we have the new reckoning. The crisis which threatened to divide the friends of the Union is passed.

" . . . In the midst of other cares, however important, we must not lose sight of the fact that the war power is still our main reliance. To that power alone can we look, yet, for a time, to give confidence to the people in the contested regions that the insurgent power will not again overrun them. Until that confidence shall be established, little can be done anywhere for what is called reconstruction. Hence, our chiefest care must still be directed to the army and navy, which have thus far borne their harder part so nobly and well. And it may be esteemed fortunate that in giving the greatest efficiency to these indispensable arms, we do also honourably recognise the gallant men, from commander to sentinel, who compose them, and to whom, more than others, the world must stand indebted for the home of freedom, disenthralled, regenerated, enlarged, and perpetuated."

CLOSING ADDRESS OF THE FAIR FOR THE SANITARY COMMISSION.

March 18, 1864.

I APPEAR to say but a word. This extraordinary war in which we are engaged falls heavily upon all classes of people, but the most heavily upon the soldier. For it has been said " all that a man hath will he give for his life ; " and while all contribute of their substance, the soldier puts his life at stake, and often yields it up in his country's cause. *The highest merit, then, is due to the soldier.*

In this extraordinary war extraordinary developments have manifested themselves, such as have not been seen in former wars ; and amongst these manifestations nothing has been more remarkable than these fairs for the relief of suffering soldiers and their families. And the chief agents in these fairs are the women of America.

I am not accustomed to the language of eulogy. I have never studied the art of paying compli-

ments to women. But I must say, that if all that
has been said by orators and poets since the
creation of the world in praise of women were
applied to the women of America, it would not
do them justice for their conduct during this
war. I will close by saying, God bless the women
of America !

LETTER TO A. G. HODGES OF KENTUCKY.

April 4, 1864.

I AM naturally anti-slavery. If slavery is not
wrong, nothing is wrong. I cannot remember
when I did not so think and feel, and yet I have
never understood that the Presidency conferred
upon me an unrestricted right to act officially
upon this judgment and feeling. It was in the
oath that I took, that I would, to the best of my
ability, preserve, protect, and defend the Constitution of the United States. I could not take
office without taking the oath. Nor was it my
view that I might take an oath to get power, and
break the oath in using the power. I understood,
too, that in ordinary civil administration this oath
even forbade me to practically indulge my primary
abstract judgment on the moral question of slavery. I had publicly declared this many times

and in many ways. And I aver that, to this day, I have done no official act in mere deference to my abstract feeling and judgment on slavery. I did understand, however, that my oath to preserve the Constitution to the best of my ability imposed upon me the duty of preserving, by every indispensable means, that government — that nation — of which that Constitution was the organic law. Was it possible to lose the nation and yet preserve the Constitution? By general law, life and limb must be protected, yet often a limb must be amputated to save a life ; but a life is never wisely given to save a limb. I felt that measures, otherwise unconstitutional, might become lawful by becoming indispensable to the preservation of the Constitution through the preservation of the nation. Right or wrong, I assumed this ground, and now avow it. I could not feel that, to the best of my ability, I had even tried to preserve the Constitution, if, to save slavery or any minor matter, I should permit the wreck of government, country, and Constitution, all together. When, early in the war, General Fremont attempted military emancipation, I forbade it, because I did not then think it an indispensable necessity. When, a little later, General Cameron, then Secretary of War, suggested the arming of the blacks, I objected, because I did not think it an indispensable necessity. When, still later, General Hunter attempted military emancipation, I again forbade it, because I did not yet think the indispensable necessity had come. When, in March and May and July, 1862, I made earnest and successive appeals to the border States to favour compensated emancipation, I believed the indispensable necessity for military emancipation and arming the blacks would come, unless averted by that measure. They declined the proposition, and I was, in my best judgment, driven to the alternative of either surrendering the Union, and with it the Constitution, or laying strong hand upon the coloured element. I chose the latter. In choosing it, I hoped for greater gain than loss; but of this I was not entirely confident. More than a year of trial now shows no loss by it in our foreign relations, none in our home popular sentiment, none in our white military force, — no loss by it anyhow or anywhere. On the contrary, it shows a gain of quite one hundred and thirty thousand soldiers, seamen, and labourers. These are palpable facts, about which, as facts, there can be no cavilling. We have the men, and we could not have had them without the measure.

And now let any Union man who complains of the measure, test himself by writing down in one line that he is for subduing the rebellion by force of arms ; and in the next, that he is for taking these hundred and thirty thousand men from the Union side, and placing them where they would be but for the measure he condemns. If he cannot face his case so stated, it is only because he cannot face the truth.

I add a word which was not in the verbal conversation. In telling this tale, I attempt no compliment to my own sagacity. I claim not to have controlled events, but confess plainly that events have controlled me. Now, at the end of three years' struggle, the nation's condition is not what either party, or any man, devised or expected. God alone can claim it. Whither it is tending seems plain. If God now wills the removal of a great wrong, and wills also that we of the North, as well as you of the South, shall pay fairly for our complicity in that wrong, impartial history will find therein new cause to attest and revere the justice and goodness of God.

His Address at the Sanitary Fair in Baltimore.

April 18, 1864.

Calling to mind that we are in Baltimore, we cannot fail to note that the world moves. Looking upon these many people, assembled here to serve, as they best may, the soldiers of the Union, it occurs at once that three years ago the same soldiers could not so much as pass through Baltimore. The change from then till now is both great and gratifying. Blessings on the brave men who have wrought the change, and the fair women who strive to reward them for it!

But Baltimore suggests more than could happen within Baltimore. The change within Baltimore is part, only, of a far wider change. When the war begun, three years ago, neither party nor any man expected it would last till now. Each looked for the end, in some way, long ere to-day. Neither did any anticipate that domestic slavery would be much affected by the war. But here we are: the war has not ended, and slavery has been much affected — how much, needs not now be recounted. So true is it that man proposes, and God disposes.

But we can see the past, though we may not

claim to have directed it; and seeing it, in this case, we feel more hopeful and confident for the future.

The world has never had a good definition of the word "liberty," and the American people, just now, are much in want of one. We all declare for liberty; but in using the same word, we do not all mean the same thing. With some, the word "liberty" may mean for each man to do as he pleases with himself and the product of his labour; while with others, the same word may mean for some men to do as they please with other men and the product of other men's labour. Here are two, not only different, but incompatible things, called by the same name, — liberty. And it follows that each of the things is, by the respective parties, called by two different and incompatible names, — liberty and tyranny.

The shepherd drives the wolf from the sheep's throat, for which the sheep thanks the shepherd as his liberator, while the wolf denounces him for the same act as the destroyer of liberty, especially as the sheep was a black one. Plainly, the sheep and the wolf are not agreed upon a definition of the word "liberty;" and precisely the same difference prevails to-day, among us human creatures, even in the North, and all professing to love liberty. Hence we behold the process by which thousands are daily passing from under the yoke of bondage hailed by some as the advance of liberty, and bewailed by others as the destruction of all liberty. Recently, as it seems, the people of Maryland have been doing something to define liberty, and thanks to them that, in what they have done, the wolf's dictionary has been repudiated.

It is not very becoming for one in my position to make speeches at great length, but there is another subject upon which I feel that I ought to say a word.

A painful rumour — true, I fear — has reached us of the massacre by the rebel forces at Fort Pillow, in the west end of Tennessee, on the Mississippi River, of some three hundred coloured soldiers and white officers, who had just been overpowered by their assailants. There seems to be some anxiety in the public mind whether the government is doing its duty to the coloured soldier, and to the service at this point. At the beginning of the war, and for some time, the use of coloured troops was not contemplated; and how the change of purpose was wrought, I will not now take time to explain. Upon a clear conviction of duty, I resolved to turn that element of strength to account; and I am responsible for it to the American people, to the Christian world, to history, and, in my final account, to God. Having determined to use the negro as a soldier, there is no way but to give him all the protection given to any other soldier. The difficulty is not in stating the principle, but in practically applying it. It is a mistake to suppose the government is indifferent to this matter, or is not doing the best it can in regard to it. We do not to-day know that a coloured soldier, or white officer commanding coloured soldiers, has been massacred by the rebels when made a prisoner. We fear it — believe it, I may say — but we do not know it. To take the life of one of their prisoners on the assumption that they murder ours, when it is short of certainty that they do murder ours, might be too serious, too cruel, a mistake. We are having the Fort Pillow affair thoroughly investigated ; and such investigation will probably show conclusively how the truth is. If after all that has been said, it shall turn out that there has been no massacre at Fort Pillow, it will be almost safe to say that there has been none, and will be none, elsewhere. If there has been the massacre of three hundred there, or even the tenth part of three hundred, it will be conclusively proved ; and

22

being so proved, the retribution shall as surely come. It will be matter of grave consideration in what exact course to apply the retribution; but in the case supposed, it must come.

His Letter to General Grant.

April 30, 1864.

NOT expecting to see you again before the spring campaign opens, I wish to express in this way my entire satisfaction with what you have done up to this time, so far as I understand it. The particulars of your plans I neither know nor seek to know. You are vigilant and self-reliant; and, pleased with this, I wish not to obtrude any constraints nor restraints upon you. While I am very anxious that any great disaster or capture of our men in great numbers shall be avoided, I know these points are less likely to escape your attention than they would be mine. If there is anything wanting which is within my power to give, do not fail to let me know it. And now, with a brave army and a just cause, may God sustain you.

His Answer to a Methodist Delegation.

May 14, 1864.

Gentlemen, — In response to your address, allow me to attest the accuracy of its historical statements, indorse the sentiments it expresses, and thank you in the nation's name for the sure promise it gives.

Nobly sustained as the government has been by all the churches, I would utter nothing that might seem invidious against any. Yet without this it may fairly be said that the Methodist Episcopal Church, not less devoted than the best, is by its greater number the most important of all. It is no fault in others that the Methodist Church sends more soldiers to the field, more nurses to the hospital, and more prayers to Heaven than any. Bless all the churches; and blessed be God who, in this our great trial, giveth us the churches.

REPLY TO A DELEGATION FROM THE UNION
LEAGUE AFTER HIS RENOMINATION.

June 9, 1864.

I CAN only say in response to the kind remarks
of your chairman, that I am very grateful for the
renewed confidence which has been accorded to
me, both by the convention and by the National
League.   I am not insensible at all to the personal compliment there is in this, and yet I do
not allow myself to believe that any but a small
portion of it is to be appropriated as a personal
compliment to me.   The convention and the
nation, I am assured, are alike animated by a
higher view of the interests of the country for the
present and the great future; and the part I am
entitled to appropriate as a compliment is only
that part which I may lay hold of as being the
opinion of the convention and of the League,
that I am not entirely unworthy to be entrusted
with the place which I have occupied for the last
three years.   I have not permitted myself to conclude that I am the best man in America; but I
am reminded in this connection of a story of an
old Dutch farmer who remarked to a companion
that " it is not best to swap horses while crossing
the stream."

From his Address at a Fair of the Sanitary Commission in Philadelphia.

June 16, 1864.

" . . . Yet the war continues, and several relieving coincidents have accompanied it from the beginning, which have not been known, as I understand or have any knowledge of, in any former wars in the history of the world. The Sanitary Commission with all its benevolent labours; the Christian Commission with all its Christian and benevolent labours; and the various places, arrangements, and institutions have contributed to the comfort and relief of the soldiers. . . . The motive and object that lie at the bottom of all these are most worthy; for, say what you will, after all, the most is due to the soldier who takes his life in his hands and goes to fight the battles of his country. . . .

" It is a pertinent question, often asked in the mind privately, and from one to the other, when is this war to end? Surely I feel as deep an interest in this question as any other can; but I do not wish to name a day, a month, or a year when it is to end. I do not wish to run any risk of seeing the time come without our being ready for the end, for fear of disappointment because the time had come and not the end. We accepted this war for an object, a worthy object, and the war will end when that object is attained. Under God, I hope it never will end until that time. Speaking of the present campaign, General Grant is reported to have said, " I am going through on this line if it takes all summer." This war has taken three years ; it was begun or accepted upon the line of restoring the national authority over the whole national domain ; and for the American people, as far as my knowledge enables me to speak, I say we are going through on this line if it takes three years more !

" My friends, I did not know but that I might be called upon to say a few words before I got away from here, but I did not know it was coming just here. I have never been in the habit of making predictions in regard to the war, but I am almost tempted to make one. If I were to hazard it, it is this : that Grant is this evening, with General Meade and General Hancock and the brave officers and soldiers with him, in a position from whence he will never be dislodged until Richmond is taken ; and I have but one single proposition to put now, and perhaps I can best put it in the form of an interrogative. If I shall discover that General Grant and the noble officers and men under him can be greatly facilitated in their work by a sudden pouring forward of men and assistance, will you give them to me? Are you ready to march? [Cries of, Yes!] Then I say, stand ready, for I am watching for the chance."

REMARKS TO THE 164th OHIO REGIMENT.

August 18, 1864.

" . . . There is more involved in this contest than is realised by every one. There is involved in this struggle the question whether your children and my children shall enjoy the privileges we have enjoyed. I say this in order to impress upon you, if you are not already so impressed, that no small matter should divert us from our great purpose.

" There may be some inequalities in the practical application of our system. It is fair that each man shall pay taxes in exact proportion to the value of his property; but if we should wait, before collecting a tax, to adjust the taxes upon each man in exact proportion with every other man, we should never collect any tax at all. There may be mistakes made sometimes; things may be done wrong, while the officers of the

government do all they can to prevent mistakes.
But I beg of you as citizens of this great Republic, not to let your minds be carried off from this
great work we have before us.   This struggle is
too large for you to be diverted from it by any
small matter.   When you return to your homes,
rise up to the height of a generation of men
worthy of a free government, and we will carry
out the great work we have commenced."

HIS LETTER TO MRS. ELIZA P. GURNEY.

September 4, 1864.

MY ESTEEMED FRIEND, — I have not forgotten — probably never shall forget — the very im-
pressive occasion when yourself and friends
visited me on a Sabbath forenoon, two years ago.
Nor has your kind letter, written nearly a year
later, ever been forgotten.   In all, it has been
your purpose to strengthen my reliance on God.
I am much indebted to the good Christian people
of the country for their constant prayers and con-
solations ; and to no one of them more than to
yourself.   The purposes of the Almighty are perfect, and must prevail, though we erring mortals
may fail to accurately perceive them in advance.
We hoped for a happy termination of this terrible

war long before this; but God knows best, and has ruled otherwise. We shall yet acknowledge His wisdom and our own error therein. Meanwhile we must work earnestly, in the best lights He gives us, trusting that so working still conduces to the great ends He ordains. Surely He intends some great good to follow this mighty convulsion, which no mortal could make, and no mortal could stay. Your people, the Friends, have had and are having a very great trial. On principle and faith opposed to both war and oppression, they can only practically oppose oppression by war. In this hard dilemma, some have chosen one horn, and some the other. For those appealing to me on conscientious grounds, I have done and shall do the best I could and can, in my own conscience, under my oath to the law. That you believe this, I doubt not; and believing it, I shall still receive for our country and myself your earnest prayers to Our Father in Heaven.

To the Coloured Men of Baltimore for a Present of the Bible.

September 7, 1864.

". . . I can only now say, as I have often before said, it has always been a sentiment with me that all mankind should be free. So far as able, within my sphere, I have always acted as I believe to be right and just; and I have done all I could for the good of mankind, generally. In letters and documents sent from this office, I have expressed myself better than I now can. In regard to this Great Book, I have but to say it is the best gift God has given to man.

"All the good the Saviour gave to the world was communicated through this Book. But for it, we could not know right from wrong. All things most desirable for man's welfare, here and hereafter, are to be found portrayed in it. To you I return my most sincere thanks for the very elegant copy of the great Book of God which you present."

His Reply to a Serenade.

October 19, 1864.

I AM notified that this is a compliment paid me by the loyal Marylanders resident in this District. I infer that the adoption of the new constitution for the State furnishes the occasion, and that, in your view, the extirpation of slavery constitutes the chief merit of the new constitution. Most heartily do I congratulate you and Maryland, and the nation and the world, upon this event. I regret that it did not occur two years sooner, which, I am sure, would have saved the nation more money than would have met all the private loss incident to the measure ; but it has come at last, and I sincerely hope its friends may fully realise all their anticipations of good from it, and that its opponents may by its effects be agreeably and profitably disappointed.

A word upon another subject. Something said by the Secretary of State, in his recent speech at Auburn, has been construed by some into a threat that if I shall be beaten at the election, I will, between then and the end of my constitutional term, do what I may be able to ruin the government. Others regard the fact that the Chicago Convention adjourned, not *sine die*, but to meet again, if called to do so by a particular individual, as the intimation of a purpose that if their nominee shall be elected, he will at once seize the control of the government. I hope the good people will permit themselves to suffer no uneasiness on either point.

I am struggling to maintain the government, not to overthrow it. I am struggling, especially, to prevent others from overthrowing it. I therefore say, that if I shall live, I shall remain President until the 4th of next March; and that whoever shall be constitutionally elected therefor in November, shall be duly installed as President on the 4th of March; and that, in the interval, I shall do my utmost that whoever is to hold the helm for the next voyage shall start with the best possible chance to save the ship.

This is due to the people, both on principle and under the Constitution. Their will, constitutionally expressed, is the ultimate law for all. If they should deliberately resolve to have immediate peace, even at the loss of their country and their liberty, I know not the power or the right to resist them. It is their own business, and they must do as they please with their own. I believe, however, they are still resolved to preserve their country and their liberty; and in this, in office or out of it, I am resolved to stand by them.

I may add that in this purpose — to save the country and its liberties — no classes of people seem so nearly unanimous as the soldiers in the field and the sailors afloat. Do they not have the hardest of it? Who should quail when they do not? God bless the soldiers and seamen, with all their brave commanders.

His Reply to a Serenade when his Re-election was certain.

November 10, 1864.

It has long been a grave question whether any government not too strong for the liberties of its people, can be strong enough to maintain its existence in great emergencies. On this point the present rebellion brought our Republic to a severe test; and a presidential election, occurring in regular course during the rebellion, added not a little to the strain.

If the loyal people united were put to the utmost of their strength by the rebellion, must they not fail when divided and partially paralysed by a political war among themselves? But the election was a necessity. We cannot have free government without elections; and if the rebellion could force us to forego or postpone a national election, it might fairly claim to have already conquered and ruined us. The strife of the election is but human nature practically applied to the facts of the case. What has occurred in this case must ever occur in similar cases. Human nature will not change. In any future great national trial, compared with the men of this, we shall have as weak and as strong, as silly and as wise, as bad and as good. Let us, therefore, study the incidents of this as philosophy to learn wisdom from, and none of them as wrongs to be revenged. But the election, along with its incidental and undesirable strife, has done good, too. It has demonstrated that a people's government can sustain a national election in the midst of a great civil war. Until now, it has not been known to the world that this was a possibility. It shows also how sound and how strong we still are. It shows that, even among candidates of the same party, he who is most devoted to the Union and most opposed to treason can receive most of the people's votes. It shows also, to the extent yet known, that we have more men now than we had when the war began.

Gold is good in its place, but living, brave, patriotic men are better than gold.

But the rebellion continues; and now that the election is over, may not all having a common interest reunite in a common effort to save our common country? For my own part, I have striven and shall strive to avoid placing any obstacle in the way. So long as I have been here, I have not willingly planted a thorn in any man's bosom. While I am deeply sensible to the high compliment of a re-election, and duly grateful as I trust to Almighty God for having directed my countrymen to a right conclusion, as I think, for their own good, it adds nothing to my satisfaction that any other man may be disappointed or pained by the result.

May I ask those who have not differed with me, to join with me in this same spirit towards those who have? And now let me close by asking three hearty cheers for our brave soldiers and seamen, and their gallant and skilful commanders.

His Letter to Mrs. Bixby.

November 21, 1864.

Dear Madam, — I have been shown in the files of the War Department a statement of the Adjutant General of Massachusetts, that you are the mother of five sons who have died gloriously on the field of battle.   I feel how weak and fruitless must be any words of mine which should attempt to beguile you from a loss so overwhelming.   But I cannot refrain from tendering to you the consolation that may be found in the thanks of the Republic they died to save.   I pray that our Heavenly Father may assuage the anguish of your bereavement, and leave you only the cherished memory of the loved and lost, and the solemn pride that must be yours to have laid so costly a sacrifice upon the Altar of Freedom.

From his Annual Message to Congress.

December 6, 1864.

". . . The ports of Norfolk, Fernandina, and Pensacola have been opened by proclamation.   It is hoped that foreign merchants will now consider whether it is not safer and more profitable to themselves, as well as just to the United States, to resort to these and other open ports, than it is to pursue, through many hazards and at vast cost, a contraband trade with other ports which are closed, if not by actual military occupation, at least by a lawful and effective blockade.

"For myself, I have no doubt of the power and duty of the Executive, under the law of nations, to exclude enemies of the human race from an asylum in the United States. If Congress should think that proceedings in such cases lack the authority of law, or ought to be further regulated by it, I recommend that provision be made for effectually preventing foreign slave-traders from acquiring domicile and facilities for their criminal occupation in our country.

"It is possible that if it were a new and open question, the maritime powers, with the lights they now enjoy, would not concede the privileges of a naval belligerent to the insurgents of the United States, destitute as they are, and always have been, equally of ships of war and of ports and harbours. Disloyal emissaries have been neither less assiduous nor more successful, during the last year, than they were before that time in their efforts, under favour of that privilege, to embroil our country in foreign wars. The desire and the determination of the governments of the

23

maritime States to defeat that design, are believed to be as sincere as, and cannot be more earnest than, our own.

" . . . It is of noteworthy interest, that the steady expansion of population, improvement, and governmental institutions over the new and unoccupied portions of our country have scarcely been checked, much less impeded or destroyed, by our great civil war, which at first glance would seem to have absorbed almost the entire energies of the nation.

" . . . The war continues. Since the last annual message all the important lines and positions then occupied by our forces have been maintained, and our arms have steadily advanced, thus liberating the regions left in their rear; so that Missouri, Kentucky, Tennessee, and parts of other States have again produced reasonably fair crops.

"The most remarkable feature in the military operations of the year is General Sherman's attempted march of three hundred miles, directly through the insurgent region. It tends to show a great increase of our relative strength, that our general-in-chief should feel able to confront and hold in check every active force of the enemy, and yet to detach a well-appointed, large army to move on such an expedition. The result not yet being known, conjecture in regard to it is not here indulged.

". . . The most reliable indication of public purpose in this country is derived through our popular elections. Judging by the recent canvass and its result, the purpose of the people, within the loyal States, to maintain the integrity of the Union, was never more nearly unanimous than now. The extraordinary calmness and good order with which millions of voters met and mingled at the polls give strong assurance of this. Not only all those who supported the Union ticket, so called, but a great majority of the opposing party also, may be fairly claimed to entertain and to be actuated by the same purpose. It is an unanswerable argument to this effect, that no candidate for any office, high or low, has ventured to seek votes on the avowal that he was for giving up the Union.

". . . The election has exhibited another fact not less valuable to be known, — the fact that we do not approach exhaustion in the most important branch of national resources, that of living men. While it is melancholy to reflect that the war has filled so many graves, and carried mourning to so many hearts, it is some relief to know, that compared with the surviving the fallen have been so few. While corps, divisions, and brigades and regiments have formed and fought, and dwindled and gone out of existence, a great majority of the men who composed them are still living. The election returns prove this. The States regularly holding elections, both now and four years ago, viz., . . . show a net increase, during three years and a half of war, of 145,551 votes.

"... It is not material to inquire how the increase has been produced, or to show that it would have been greater but for the war; which is probably true. The important fact remains demonstrated, that we have more men now than we had when the war began; that we are not exhausted nor in process of exhaustion; that we are gaining strength, and may, if need be, maintain the contest indefinitely. This as to men. Material resources are now more complete and abundant than ever.

"The national resources, then, are unexhausted, and, as we believe, inexhaustible. The public purpose to re-establish and maintain the national authority is unchanged, and, as we believe, unchangeable. The manner of continuing the effort remains to choose. On careful consideration of all the evidence accessible, it seems to me that no attempt at negotiation with the insurgent leader could result in any good. He would accept nothing short of severance of the Union, — precisely what we will not and cannot give.

" . . . Between him and us the issue is distinct, simple, and inflexible. It is an issue which can only be tried by war and decided by victory. If we yield, we are beaten. If the Southern people fail him, he is beaten. Either way, it would be the victory and defeat following war.

" . . . In presenting the abandonment of armed resistance to the national authority on the part of the insurgents as the only indispensable condition to ending the war on the part of the government, I retract nothing heretofore said as to slavery. I repeat the declaration made a year ago, that ' while I remain in my present position I shall not attempt to retract or modify the Emancipation Proclamation, nor shall I return to slavery any person who is free by the terms of that proclamation, or by any of the Acts of Congress.'

" If the people should, by whatever mode or means, make it an Executive duty to re-enslave such persons, another, and not I, must be their instrument to perform it.

"In stating a single condition of peace, I mean simply to say, that the war will cease on the part of the government whenever it shall have ceased on the part of those who began it."

THE SECOND INAUGURAL ADDRESS.

March 4, 1865.

FELLOW-COUNTRYMEN : At this second appearing to take the oath of the Presidential office, there is less occasion for an extended address than there was at the first. Then a statement, somewhat in detail, of a course to be pursued, seemed fitting and proper. Now, at the expiration of four years, during which public declarations have been constantly called forth on every point and phase of the great contest which still absorbs the attention and engrosses the energies of the nation, little that is new could be presented. The progress of our arms, upon which all else chiefly depends, is as well known to the public as to myself; and it is, I trust, reasonably satisfactory and encouraging to all. With high hope for the future, no prediction in regard to it is ventured.

On the occasion corresponding to this four

years ago, all thoughts were anxiously directed to
an impending civil war. All dreaded it, — all
sought to avert it. While the inaugural address
was being delivered from this place, devoted
altogether to saving the Union without war, insurgent agents were in the city seeking to destroy
it without war, — seeking to dissolve the Union,
and divide effects, by negotiation. Both parties
deprecated war; but one of them would make
war rather than let the nation survive, and the
other would accept war rather than let it perish.
And the war came.

One eighth of the whole population were
coloured slaves, not distributed generally over
the Union, but localized in the southern part
of it. These slaves constituted a peculiar and
powerful interest. All knew that this interest was,
somehow, the cause of the war. To strengthen,
perpetuate, and extend this interest was the object
for which the insurgents would rend the Union,
even by war; while the government claimed no
right to do more than to restrict the territorial
enlargement of it.

Neither party expected for the war the magnitude or the duration which it has already attained. Neither anticipated that the cause of
the conflict might cease with, or even before,

the conflict itself should cease. Each looked for
an easier triumph and a result less fundamental
and astounding. Both read the same Bible, and
pray to the same God; and each invokes His
aid against the other. It may seem strange
that any men should dare to ask a just God's
assistance in wringing their bread from the sweat
of other men's faces; but let us judge not, that
we be not judged. The prayers of both could
not be answered — that of neither has been
answered fully.

The Almighty has His own purposes. "Woe
unto the world because of offences! for it must
needs be that offences come; but woe to that
man by whom the offence cometh." If we shall
suppose that American slavery is one of those
offences which, in the Providence of God, must
needs come, but which having continued through
His appointed time, He now wills to remove, and
that He gives to both North and South this
terrible war, as the woe due to those by whom
the offence came, shall we discern therein any
departure from those divine attributes which the
believers in a living God always ascribe to Him?
Fondly do we hope — fervently do we pray —
that this mighty scourge of war may speedily
pass away. Yet, if God wills that it continue

until all the wealth piled by the bondman's two hundred and fifty years of unrequited toil shall be sunk, and until every drop of blood drawn by the lash shall be paid by another drawn with the sword, as was said three thousand years ago, so still it must be said, "The judgments of the Lord are true and righteous altogether."

With malice toward none; with charity for all; with firmness in the right, as God gives us to see the right, — let us strive on to finish the work we are in: to bind up the nation's wounds; to care for him who shall have borne the battle, and for his widow and his orphan; to do all which may achieve and cherish a just and lasting peace among ourselves, and with all nations.

FROM HIS ANSWER TO A SERENADE — HIS
LAST PUBLIC ADDRESS.

April 11, 1865.

"FELLOW-CITIZENS: We meet this evening, not in sorrow but in gladness of heart. The evacuation of Richmond and Petersburg, and the surrender of the principal insurgent army, give the hope of a just and speedy peace, the joyous expression of which cannot be restrained. In all this joy, however, HE from whom all blessings flow must not be forgotten. A call for a national thanksgiving is in the course of preparation, and will be duly promulgated. Nor must those whose harder part give us the cause for rejoicing be overlooked. Their honours must not be parcelled out with others. I, myself, was near the front, and had the high pleasure of transmitting much of the good news to you ; but no part of the honour for plan or execution is mine. To General Grant, his skilful officers and brave men, all belongs. The gallant navy stood ready, but was not in reach to take an active part.

" By these recent successes the reinauguration of the national authority, — reconstruction, — which has had a large share of thought from the first, is pressed much more closely upon our attention. It is fraught with great difficulty. Unlike a case of war between independent nations, there is no organized organ for us to treat with, — no one man has authority to give up the rebellion for any other man. We simply must begin with and mould from disorganized and discordant elements. Nor is it a small additional embarrassment that we, the loyal people, differ among ourselves as to the mode, manner, and measure of reconstruction. As a general rule I abstain from reading the reports of attacks upon myself, wishing not to be provoked by that to which I cannot properly offer an answer. In spite of this precaution, however, it comes to my knowledge that I am much censured for some supposed agency in setting up and seeking to sustain the new State government of Louisiana.

In this I have done just so much as, and no more than, the public knows. In the annual message of December, 1863, and in the accompanying proclamation, I presented a plan of reconstruction, as the phrase goes, which I promised, if adopted by any State, should be acceptable to and sustained by the executive government of the nation. I distinctly stated that this was not the only plan which might possibly be acceptable, and I also distinctly protested that the executive claimed no right to say when or whether members should be admitted to seats in Congress from such States. This plan was in advance submitted to the then Cabinet, and approved by every member of it. . . .

"We all agree that the seceded States, so called, are out of their proper, practical relation with the Union, and that the sole object of the government, civil and military, in regard to those States, is to again get them into that proper practical relation. I believe that it is not only possible, but in fact easier, to do this without deciding or even considering whether these States have ever been out of the Union, than with it. Finding themselves safely at home, it would be utterly immaterial whether they had ever been abroad. Let us all join in doing the acts necessary to restoring the proper practical relations between these States and the Union, and each forever after innocently indulge his own opinion whether in doing the acts he brought the States from without into the Union, or only gave them proper assistance, they never having been out of it. The amount of constituency, so to speak, on which the new Louisiana government rests, would be more satisfactory to all if it contained fifty thousand, or thirty thousand, or even twenty thousand, instead of only about twelve thousand, as it does. It is also unsatisfactory to some that the elective franchise is not given to the coloured man. I would myself prefer that it were now conferred on the very intelligent, and on those who serve our cause as soldiers.

" Still, the question is not whether the Louisiana government, as it stands, is quite all that is desirable. The question is, will it be wiser to take it as it is and help to improve it, or to reject and

disperse it? Can Louisiana be brought into
proper practical relation with the Union sooner
by sustaining or by discarding her new State
government? Some twelve thousand voters in
the heretofore slave State of Louisiana have sworn
allegiance to the Union, assumed to be the rightful political power of the State, held elections,
organised a State government, adopted a free-
State constitution, giving the benefit of public
schools equally to black and white, and empower-
ing the legislature to confer the elective franchise
upon the coloured man. Their legislature has
already voted to ratify the constitutional amendment recently passed by Congress, abolishing
slavery throughout the nation. These twelve
thousand persons are thus fully committed to the
Union and to perpetual freedom in the State, —
committed to the very things, and nearly all the
things, the nation wants, — and they ask the
nation's recognition and its assistance to make
good their committal.

" If we reject and spurn them, we do our
utmost to disorganise and disperse them. We, in
effect, say to the white man: You are worthless
or worse ; we will neither help you, nor be helped
by you. To the blacks, we say : This cup of liberty, which these, your old masters, hold to your

lips, we will dash from you, and leave you to the chances of gathering the spilled and scattered contents in some vague and undefined when, where, and how. If this course, discouraging and paralysing both white and black, has any tendency to bring Louisiana into proper, practical relations with the Union, I have so far been unable to perceive it. If, on the contrary, we recognise and sustain the new government, the converse of all this is made true. . . .

" . . . What has been said of Louisiana will apply generally to other States. And yet so great peculiarities pertain to each State, and such important and sudden changes occur in the same State, and withal so new and unprecedented is the whole case, that no exclusive and inflexible plan can safely be prescribed as to details and collaterals. Such exclusive and inflexible plan would surely become a new entanglement. Important principles may and must be inflexible. In the present situation, as the phrase goes, it may be my duty to make some new announcement to the people of the South. I am considering, and shall not fail to act when satisfied that action will be proper."